HUMAN RESOURCE MANAGEMENT

IN

SMALL LIBRARIES

HUMAN RESOURCE MANAGEMENT

IN

SMALL LIBRARIES

Beverly A. Rawles

Library Professional Publications

1982

© 1982 Battelle Memorial Institute
All rights reserved
First published in 1982
as a Library Professional Publication,
an imprint of The Shoe String Press, Inc.,
Hamden, CT 06514
Printed in the United States of America

Library of Congress Cataloging in Publication Data
Rawles, Beverly A.
Main entry under title: Human resource management
in small libraries.
Includes bibliographies and index.
1. Library personnel management   United States.
I. Title
Z682.2.U5R38   023'.9   81-20834
ISBN 0-208-01966-9   AACR2
ISBN 0-208-01950-2 (pbk.)

CONTENTS

Preface   vii
Introduction   ix
1. Issues and Trends   1
2. Developing a Management Philosophy   11
3. Transition to Management   17
4. Communicating with the Staff   27
5. The Manager as Supervisor   37
6. Staff Development   43
7. Performance Appraisal   57
8. Compensation   65
9. Equal Employment Opportunity and Affirmative Action   77
10. Labor Relations   95
11. School Library Media Centers   105
Appendixes   121
Index   129

PREFACE

PREFACE

This book has been written to guide the new or inexperienced director of a small library, who must come to grips very quickly with many aspects of management, through the first year on the job.

The most valuable resource of the library—its staff—requires the attention of the new administrator almost as soon as the ink is dry on his or her contract. On the premise that administrative success is far less dependent on budgeting, organization and control than on affirmative action, staff development and deployment, performance appraisal, salary administration, and communications, the latter have been made the foci of this book. Planning, budgeting, and programming are treated as they relate to these topics and to the librarian's management of his or her own time and talents.

Many of the ideas and suggestions presented stem from the author's experience and the experience of other librarians; others come from the literature of management, and an effort has been made to adapt them to application in libraries.

The managers of small libraries, public, school, and special, are the audience. Some material, however, is not limited in applicability to small libraries, notably the chapter on equal employment opportunity and affirmative action.

School library media centers are treated in a separate chapter, since they differ in important respects from the two other types of libraries. The school librarian or media specialist will also find much adaptable information in the other chapters of this book, however.

Although not specifically written as a text, the book may be of help to students of library science who are preparing for positions in library administration and is designed to be useful as collateral reading for library courses. The annotated bibliography at the end of each chapter refers to books and articles that treat the subject in more depth and detail. They are recommended to those who require more information.

My thanks go to Professor William Dowling for reading the text and encouraging me to complete this work; to Martha Korns, who reviewed the manuscript and made helpful suggestions; to my students, whose desire to learn stimulates me; and to Eleanor Kilgour for tireless editorial assistance.

Beverly A. Rawles
June, 1981

INTRODUCTION

This book is based on two premises: in the closing decades of this century personnel management will be different from the past; and library managers will need to take cognizance of the changing economic, technological, and social conditions that require new management skills and styles.

Controlling inflation will continue to be a major concern of government and the taxpayers. The energy shortages that fuel inflation will also limit the mobility and buying power of people, particularly older people, a group already requiring improved and expanded library services as their numbers and educational levels rise. Library operating costs will grow with the spiraling prices of materials, utilities, building maintenance, and salaries. The service society of the post-industrial era will make heavy and "instant" information demands on libraries (Becker 1980).

With respect to the technological revolution, libraries are in their infancy. The decreasing costs of computers will soon enable even small libraries, individually or as network members, to enjoy the benefits of computerization of mechanical functions such as acquisitions, cataloging, circulation, and literature searching. The library manager will need to employ, develop, and train staff who can keep pace with technological advances, and administrators will have to cope with the adjustment problems of some staff members when they use computer terminals and other electronic equipment for the first time.

Many social changes—the end of mandatory retirement, the rising median age of the population, the new and updated skills demanded of adult workers, the pressing for equality from minorities and women, declining birth rate and school enrollment, and the changes effected by legislation and government regulations—all will affect the way libraries are managed, their service priorities, and the kinds of skills their staffs must have (Drucker 1980).

Librarians will become increasingly concerned about the needs of people. Over the next few decades they will have unprecedented professional challenges and opportunities.

Public libraries' traditional service—the provision of educational, recreational, and cultural reading and children's programs—has broadened into a service that includes information in new formats and useful to many new groups—homebound, institutionalized, handicapped, and those for whom English is a second language, among others. Some of this change can be attributed to the availability of federal funds for libraries and to state and local governments' willingness to increase their funding to support library services.

In addition, hundreds of library buildings have been constructed with the help of funds provided by the Library Services and Construction Act of 1964. The result is that many communities have good quality library services for the first time and others are enjoying vastly enlarged and improved library services.

Public libraries are actively assessing their communities' information needs and offering services unthought-of twenty years ago. They are also finding that as the average citizen becomes more aware of the value of his library he demands more of it. Use begets more use. The public service arena in which the public library now operates requires that it publicize its services, compete for budget, and muster political and public support along with other educational, as well as health, police, fire, and welfare agencies.

The public library manager is in most instances an employee of local government, and as such represents the library to other agencies and to the public in respect to planning, budgeting, and providing services. Because the library is an integral part of the community structure, its manager must take the initiative to become involved in these activities, and to interact with other agencies of government.

The special library manager in business or industry is in an analogous situation. He or she represents the library to other components of the organization and must be involved in planning, budgeting, and problem solving for the whole enterprise. It is particularly incumbent on the special librarian to anticipate, as well as to meet, the organization's information needs; this means taking the initiative, by survey and personal contacts, to ascertain what those needs will be. The manager of a special library must develop, just as the public librarian must, the capacity to work effectively and positively with management counterparts and potential library users.

The manager of a school library media center is working in an area that is still evolving professionally, while facing the paradoxical situation of decreasing clientele and budgets. Elementary and secondary school populations are, for the moment, in decline. Although they are likely to increase again, by that time the locations and methods of instruction and learning will have changed. The school library media program manager must meet this complex challenge by working more closely with teachers to ensure integration of library media center use with classroom and independent learning while reaching out to new community users of other than school age (Baker 1979).

The movements of the past two decades—civil rights, feminism, anti-war, equality for minorities, pro-gay, environmental protection, and others—have changed the perceptions and behaviors of entire segments of the population. People are striving for acceptance, dignity, and fuller participation in the decisions that control their lives. They want more from their jobs than titles and paychecks.

Managers also expect more satisfaction from their work and want jobs that offer challenge. They too wish to be productive, to make a contribution, and to receive recognition for their efforts. These mutual needs of manager and managed can only be met if there is communication, trust, and cooperation on both sides.

The new times demand that old-fashioned, top-down management that stifles employee initiative be replaced with a style of management that encourages individual growth and worker participation. The library manager who can delegate responsibility and share major decisions with the staff will strengthen the library by developing people on its staff who are enthusiastic about its mission (Sinetar 1980), and feel a sense of responsibility for satisfying the informational needs of users.

BIBLIOGRAPHY

Baker, D. Philip. "School Libraries and Media Programs." In *The ALA Yearbook 1980*. Chicago: American Library Association, 1979, pp. 276-280.

Library media specialists are trying new ways to deliver services, seeking new users in the face of declining enrollments, and would like to base staffing requirements and budgets on the number of programs provided rather than per capita enrollments. Space requirements for media centers are being reassessed and there is less emphasis on whether practitioners are called media specialists or librarians.

Becker, Joseph. "New Departures in Scientific and Technical Information." In *Perspectives on Scientific and Technical Information*. Proceedings of a Conference, Oak Ridge National Laboratory, Oak Ridge, TN, September 9-10, 1980, in press.

A forecast that covers networking, sharing of resources, technological development, and communications. The "book" is predicted to stay because it is a convenient package and adaptable to many situations.

Drucker, Peter F. *Managing in Turbulent Times*. New York: Harper & Row Publishers, 1980.

A turbulent future will require managers who can ensure that their institutions will have the capacity to survive any blow, adapt to change, and take advantage of opportunities. Effective utilization of human resources is gained by assigning people where the application of their strengths can produce results and where they have opportunities to grow. Workers must be challenged to improve what they are doing. Supervisors must be willing to consult their workers and to listen to them; the skilled worker knows more about his job than anyone else in the organization.

Sinetar, Marsha. "Management in the New Age: An Exploration of Changing Work Values." *Personnel Journal* 59 (September 1980): 749-755.

Prescribes that people, groups, and governments work cooperatively rather than competitively. New problems and many changes must be dealt with by management in all organizations: energy shortages; the nuclear threat; new technologies in communications, transport, and the military.

1

ISSUES AND TRENDS

TRENDS

There are a number of trends which are already making an impact on the way libraries manage their human resources: the development of an increasingly intensive technical environment, the sophisticated needs and wants of the staff, inflation, changing emphasis in library services, and the changes in education for librarianship.

THE TECHNOLOGICAL ENVIRONMENT

In the 1980's the computer continues to dominate technological changes in libraries. The rapid development of computer equipment results in decreasing the costs of storing information and increasing the speed of access, enabling libraries to buy this capability and use it to improve efficiency of operations and services to users. Computer technology has brought with it the need for training of library employees in its use throughout the organization. This trend will continue as new equipment and new applications of computers appear; the effectiveness of the technology is directly dependent upon the adequacy of training. These training needs will be reflected in library school curricula, increasing numbers of workshops and seminars, and more extensive on-the-job training.

Libraries are already providing home delivery of information electronically. Still, on-site use of libraries will increase, but it will not be measured by counting the number of people who pass through the front door. Librarians must become knowledge specialists on a larger scale as they respond to the users' requirements for instant information. With the mechanical aspects of librarianship being handled by fewer staff members and with much greater efficiency, both the professional and nonprofessional staff can devote the major portions of their time in direct services to users. There will be an increasingly larger number of professional librarians who are both subject and bibliographic specialists.

In conjunction with computer technology, facsimile transmission, photocopy machines, and microforms will increase in use. Librarians will use computer conferencing to tap the intellectual resources of other librarians and receive desired information in electronic form for transmission to their users.

The technological revolution is yet in its infancy for libraries. Thanks to technology, these information agencies can become a major communications link in their communities, providing access to the store of knowledge accumulated over the centuries. Keeping pace with technology and cooperation in using it are the challenges of the 80's for librarianship.

NEEDS OF THE STAFF

Library managers must cope with both the impact of technological change and the growing needs of the staff for personal growth and development. Technology can increase efficiency, decrease the number of routine jobs in libraries, and free the library staff to do more interesting and meaningful work. The staff will be more sophisticated and better educated, and have higher expectations of the quality of life in the work place. They will demand meaningful and frequent interactions with managers and supervisors, freely flowing communications, and an opportunity to participate in decision making. They will not readily accept and remain in jobs that do not afford purpose to their lives and an opportunity to contribute to the advancement of their profession, and through their profession, society as a whole.

Library staff members of the 80's will be seeking jobs that help them meet their needs for self-esteem and self-fulfillment. Their lower-order survival needs will have already been met; they are not children of the Great Depression who grew up with material deprivation, but rather children of affluence who place high value on intrinsic rewards. The library manager will be challenged to help them meet these needs through participation, involvement, and contribution.

INFLATION

Controlling inflation will continue to be a major concern of all agencies and individuals in the 1980's. Energy shortages will fuel inflation. The costs of operating libraries will increase in spite of efforts to limit the rise in costs through the application of technology and sharing of resources. Library materials will continue to increase in cost, and salaries will continue to rise. Library managers will employ paraprofessionals and part-time staff wherever they can to cut costs; volunteers will be used to a greater extent, especially in small public libraries and schools. Library budgets will receive even closer scrutiny by local government, making the decade of the 80's a time of belt-tightening and frugality, and challenging managers to be able to project convincingly library relevance to social and economic priorities, and "quality of life" potential. On the brighter side, libraries will be able to deliver higher quality services, thanks to technology and better educated staff.

LIBRARY SERVICES

In a society of instant food, fast intercontinental travel, instant communications via television and telephone, it is not surprising that users of libraries expect to get information very quickly. They do not want a bibliography on the subject but the articles and books that are relevant, and preferably copies they can keep. Generally they are willing to pay for this service and appreciate the professional efforts it requires. Many are pleased that their libraries are ready, able, and willing to deliver services at such low costs.

The 1980's will see library services change and expand in scope. "Free" access to information will be recognized as a service people are willing to tax themselves to get and enjoy. The book will continue to enjoy its position of prominence in libraries, although books will be even more readily available than they are now in paperback bookstores, supermarkets, drugstores, and airport kiosks. As society becomes better educated, its members more indi-

economic, health, recreational information, and a sense of community. The aging society will require more and better services and access to materials for those with physical impairments, such as sight and hearing. Mobility for the aged will be a problem which could result in a resurgence of bookmobile and van services to provide services where they live.

The need for library services to business, industry, and government will increase. Likewise the use of libraries by students will rise. The major increase in student use will come from adults seeking resources to support their formal and self-instructional programs. Librarians will find themselves increasingly in the role of consultant and adviser to adult learners who require the help of the subject specialist in libraries. Libraries stand at the threshold of a new age of enlightenment as students of all ages recognize their potential as centers of learning.

Libraries will participate in information services to their communities via home computer and video support. Electronic delivery of information will be a great opportunity for libraries, for they already have a large store of knowledge and the expertise to select from it that portion that fills the users' needs.

EDUCATION FOR LIBRARIANSHIP

The 1970's have seen the word "information" interjected into the name of schools of library science across the country. Information science has brought mechanized storage and retrieval to libraries. Librarians have learned the skills to use this technology, and, in most cases, instead of having problems adjusting to computerized systems, they have thrived on them.

The 1980's will be a time of increasing emphasis on change in traditional library education. There will be a continuing demand from students for theory-based concepts and practices, for increased relevancy of learning to the jobs they hold already, and for the freedom to explore aspects of library and information science that interest them. Many library school graduates will be exploring new ways in which to utilize their degrees. The curricula of schools must be flexible to incorporate the experience and learning the students bring to them. It is no longer a matter of faculties prescribing courses which they believe students need based upon tradition or

vidual in their interests, thanks to continuing educational activities and television, the demand for reading material will increase.

As the population ages and the number of people over age 60 increases, library services will be required to meet their needs for past perceptions of what should be taught. Students will be the designers of their study programs, and faculty will be facilitators and resource persons. The course outline will not be finalized in advance, but will be open to student input and to modification throughout the courses. The emphases will not be on lectures and predetermined subject matter, but on student interactions with one another and the faculty. The students will grow and develop at unprecedented rates as they assume responsibility for their own learning.

Library school faculty will have new opportunities to spend sabbatical leave in libraries as management consultants or subject specialists, and practitioners will continue to be incorporated in library school faculties as visiting professors.

Library education programs, as they anticipate the changing needs of libraries, will develop courses, seminars, workshops, and other learning experiences to meet continuing education requirements. The age of technology and the growing desire of librarians for relevant learning are already stimulating library schools to provide educational programs with a high degree of flexibility and variety.

In summary, the trends are both challenging and demanding. Library directors must be willing to let go of that which is outmoded, recognize the effects of economic and political change, and draw upon the unique talents and strengths of their staffs to assist them in planning for the future and coping with the realities of the present. The challenge, the opportunities, and the excitement are unequalled by anything we have known to date.

ISSUES

There are a number of issues before the library profession at the opening of the decade of the 1980's which are staff related and which will require the time and attention of library managers: equal opportunity for jobs and promotions, equal pay for equal work and for comparable work, priorities for service in the face of budget constraints, and a definition of professionalism.

EQUAL OPPORTUNITY FOR JOBS AND PROMOTIONS

The antidiscrimination laws are already affecting the large libraries that are part of universities, and federal, state, and local governments, and the libraries of large corporations. In the future these laws will be felt increasingly by all libraries, large and small, and compliance will be required by all. There are 38 states that have their own compliance agencies, in addition to the federal ones, which means that all employers must make real efforts to offer equal opportunity to minorities, women, and the handicapped for jobs and promotions. Extra effort, or affirmative action, will be required to reverse the discriminatory practices of the past. In libraries the price of noncompliance can be loss of federal funds, grievances filed by the staff, and law suits in which damages are sought.

Library managers and their boards of trustees cannot afford to ignore the laws including the Civil Rights Act, Title VII; Equal Pay Act; Age Discrimination in Employment Act; and the various Presidential Directives as discussed in a later chapter. A knowledge of the federal, state, and local laws which apply to their libraries is mandatory if the problems associated with noncompliance are to be averted.

Library staff members want fair and equitable treatment. If enlightened managers do not provide it voluntarily, the law and labor unions will be their recourse. The nondiscrimination in employment legislation actually provides a solid basis for many personnel policies and practices such as recruitment, promotion, and staff development which should be recognized and used by library managers as they formulate their own policies. The laws essentially provide guidelines which are very useful.

EQUAL PAY FOR EQUAL WORK OR FOR COMPARABLE WORK

The decade of the 1980's will see progress toward resolution of the issues concerning equal pay. The trend is toward equal pay for men and women who work in libraries. There will be more women in top management jobs as more who are qualified become available and seek these positions.

The issue of equal pay for comparable work with comparable educational and experience requirements has already come to the attention of the Federal Equal Employment Opportunity Commission. Librarians, especially those working in local government, have felt that they have not received equal pay with other workers, such as those in liquor control and sanitation, although librarians have educational and experience requirements comparable or greater than those of these workers. This issue is likely to be determined in the courts if another resolution is not found.

The issue of comparable pay for administrative and subject specialists in large libraries is receiving the attention of the profession. The dual career ladder for librarians is important to staff development programs and to the ability of larger libraries to attract qualified subject expertise. It remains, however, and is likely to continue to be a decisive factor in the deliberations on job value and compensation, that the top management job carries more responsibility and higher risk than the jobs of specialists. For these reasons it is not likely that anyone will receive higher pay than the director or chief administrator. Middle management jobs and those of subject specialists are likely to receive comparable pay and other considerations in the future, if they do not already.

SERVICE PRIORITIES

Budget contraints will force library managers to review service priorities and needs assessments to guide them in the choices of services to be provided. Community needs will form the basis for these decisions, and citizen committees may be enlisted in the process of selection of services.

Library managers and boards will be forced to look for new sources of funds such as user fees, foundation support, and additional tax levies. Local governments have been hard pressed to meet the demand for public services; in the past, library service has not been considered of equal priority with health, sanitation, police, and fire service. In a sense, this is not likely to change, at least in places where library managers fail to keep projecting the importance of the long-term good and intellectual and spiritual—quality of life—priorities over merely physical and immediate survival ones. People can come to realize that their minds, as well as their houses, are their fortresses.

On the positive side of the money issue is the fact that people are willing to pay for a service they value. It is no longer unusual for libraries to charge user fees for some services to both individuals and businesses. Such fees do not have the negative connotations they once had.

DEFINITION OF PROFESSIONALISM

As the decade of the 1980's opens, there is still debate as to whether librarianship is a profession. Those who say it is cite such aspects of professionalism as the educational requirements, the accreditation procedure by the national association, and the institutional and service attributes of librarianship. At the same time, others say it is not a profession since some libraries are staffed by individuals who do not have a library science education or even education beyond high school to fill "professional" jobs, while some who are qualified as professional librarians do the work of nonprofessionals. Also receiving criticism are small public libraries that are unaffiliated with library systems and some special libraries, which are unable to provide quality services or meet minimum standards, yet represent the profession of librarianship in their communities and organizations. This book has been written to help the managers of these libraries solve such problems.

BIBLIOGRAPHY

Becker, Joseph. "New Departures in Scientific and Technical Information." In *Perspectives on Scientific and Technical*

Information. Proceedings of a Conference, Oak Ridge National Laboratory, Oak Ridge, TN, September 9-10, 1980.

Sinetar, M. "Management in the New Age: An Exploration of Changing Work Values." *Personnel Journal,* 59 (September 1980): 749-755.

Drucker, Peter. *Managing in Turbulent Times.* New York: Harper & Row Publishers, 1980.

2

DEVELOPING A MANAGEMENT PHILOSOPHY

The new library manager, excited by promotion and looking forward to success, has high expectations of the job. The first hectic weeks will require many decisions and adjustments, but they hold opportunities. The manager is in a position of trust; he or she has become the steward of important resources: people, dollars, materials, and facilities. The board of trustees or the school administration, as well as the staff, anticipate changes and improvements for the library as a result of the change of leadership.

The period of getting acquainted and learning new responsibilities includes the development of a management philosophy relating to the board and the staff. Some helpful advice is found among ancient records dating from the reign of Pharaoh Amenhotep:

> When your workers, oh! overseer, are about to launch upon a course of action which is not certain to succeed, involve yourself in it towards its improvement and identify with it to your superiors.
>
> When the course of action is overwhelmingly probable of success, to your superiors maintain anonymity.
>
> Thus, you will give of your best to your workers and stand ready to receive the worst from your superiors. But—fear not the worst, for you will witness the enthusiastic efforts of your subordinates as they strive for you to avoid the worst. Thus do organizations rise to great heights and human individuals grow to new statures.

Although several thousand years old, the message is timeless. It not only concerns people and caring—an excellent foundation for a management philosophy—but it speaks knowingly of the subtleties of good leadership.

The new manager brings a perspective to his or her first important administrative position that has been formed by many elements: experience of being managed as child, student, and staff librarian; needs for security and success in the past; attitudes toward work and responsibility; and assumptions about people. The manager's outlook is influenced further by expectations that the new job will meet his or her own needs for esteem and growth.

The assumptions the manager makes about people at work are a key element of his or her management philosophy. Douglas McGregor (1960), in developing his Theories X and Y, presents contrasting assumptions. Theory X, the negative view, assumes that people dislike and avoid work; consequently they must be controlled, coerced, threatened, and directed to get them to produce enough work to meet organizational objectives.

Theory Y, the positive view, holds that for most people expending effort in work is as natural as playing or resting. It assumes that most workers will utilize self-control and practice self-direction in performing work to which they are committed. It assumes, further, that given the opportunity, many workers will bring to the solution of organizational problems creativity, ingenuity, imagination, and enthusiasm. Theory Y assumes that the average human being seeks responsibility; Theory X that he will try to avoid it.

Managers who incline to Theory X will impose strict controls on staff and exclude them from decision making. The most successful managers, however, are those who have and demonstrate confidence in their staffs and ensure frequent, meaningful interactions with them. It is in this way that they encourage participation and reward good performance (Likert 1961).

The manager who tends toward the Theory Y assumptions might be presumed to be permissive and soft. To the contrary, he or she may be firm, even tough. Firmness is shown in not permitting destructive influences in the organization that can damage morale, disrupt harmony, or cause tension. Firmness is demonstrated by not allowing work habits that produce mediocrity in products or services. The good Theory Y manager is tough in dealing with waste, unfair treatment of other staff members or clientele, and poor use of human resources and potential.

The successful manager will be sensitive to the needs of the staff for growth and development. Maslow (1970) defines his theory of motivation as being based on a hierarchy of needs. He claims that people are motivated to satisfy first their basic physiological needs of hunger and thirst, progressing from these to safety and security needs, and then to the need to belong, and for love, esteem, and finally self-actualization. He argues that the lower or basic level needs must be satisfied before the individual moves up the hierarchy to the increasingly higher level and more intrinsic needs. He believes also that people develop a growing restlessness and discontent when all these basic needs are satisfied unless they are doing what they are really best suited for and have the opportunity to develop their potential and reach for their highest level of self-actualization. Library managers should recognize the signs and symptoms of poor placement and strive to provide developmental opportunities.

MANAGEMENT STYLES

From the management philosophy grows the new manager's style: autocratic, paternalistic, democratic, or some variation or combination of these. The autocrat makes all the decisions and establishes the rules for behavior on the job without consultation with or input from the staff. The paternalistic manager may consult the staff but still makes the decisions. This type of manager makes judgments for the good of the staff as a benevolent autocrat, encouraging very little communication from the bottom up (Quick 1976). The democratic manager actively seeks information from the staff on problems, exchanges ideas and really communicates with them, and then involves them in the decision making process. This manager, who holds Theory Y assumptions, wants meaningful interactions and a free exchange of information. The staff feels respected and trusted, and therefore involved in and responsible for the work results.

Today's manager must be concerned about the individual staff member's needs for job-satisfying experiences and growth. Good communication between manager and staff is essential to achieving the library's goals. The democratic management style in which the manager serves as a facilitator helping the staff achieve their goals and improving the quality of work life has been demonstrated as optimum for all concerned (Likert 1961). The objective is to create an environment as free from stress as possible and conducive to achievement and productivity. Achievement of this objective requires a workplace to which the staff want to come and where meaningful interactions with peers and managers can occur. Every individual is looking for values in his or her job that contribute to the enrichment of life. The staff members want to feel that the manager is concerned about each of them and is alert to providing them with opportunities for achievement and advancement. The work itself should be made interesting, insofar as possible, and challenging to the individual. The importance of the work and its benefit to others should be made clear to all of those who engage in it. The manager as facilitator and coach knows that some people need more guidance and direction than others, that some are more self-directed and innovative than others, and behaves accordingly. The wise manager, especially in a public service enterprise, gears management to individuals by an understanding of how to personalize incentives and rewards.

BIBLIOGRAPHY

Likert, Rensis. *New Patterns of Management.* New York: McGraw-Hill Book Co., 1961.

    Presents an analysis of the management style used by managers and supervisors who achieve the highest productivity, lowest turnover, lowest costs, and high level of employee satisfaction by the use of closely knit, interlocking work groups. The management style promotes sensitivity to people, effective communications, and mutual confidence and trust.

Maslow, Abraham H. *Motivation and Personality,* New York: Harper & Row, Publishers, Inc., 1970. Second Edition.

McGregor, Douglas. *The Human Side of Enterprise* New York: McGraw-Hill Book Co., 1960.

Quick, Thomas L. *Understanding People at Work; A Manager's Guide to the Behavioral Sciences.* New York: Executive Enterprises Publications Co., Inc., 1976.

    Management should find ways to help employees reach their personal work objectives through the attainment of organizational goals. Management styles are discussed: the autocratic, where the manager keeps the power and makes all decisions; the democratic, where the manager shares power by inviting subordinates to have a say in matters that affect them; and the laissez-faire, where the manager lets employees have free rein. Effective organizations permit people to have a voice in their work and in organizational decisions that affect it.

3

TRANSITION TO MANAGEMENT

The librarian selected for a top management position in a small or medium-sized library may come to it quite unprepared, by previous training or experience, for its demands. The new manager often comes from a staff job, and, although knowing the work in general, knows little about the overall organization of it. He or she may even come from a job outside the library, such as teaching, that imposed limited or different responsibilities and demanded other skills. While enjoying the increased prestige and opportunity for self-development that the position offers, the new manager must quickly adapt to and learn to handle effectively the greater demands it makes.

The newly appointed manager must recognize from the outset the most significant difference between the old job and the new: whereas the former entailed responsibility for only one or two library functions, the latter embraces the ultimate responsibility for all functions, for all the personnel performing them, and for their integration into a responsive service organization.

The coordinating, unifying role is the manager's most important one, but, additionally, the manager must be the principal representative of the library in the community or in the parent organization; the chief interpreter of policies and procedures on behalf of the board of trustees; and the principal decision maker with respect to the management of the library's most important resources: staff, books, money, and equipment (Shaughnessy 1979).

Planning and organizing for the best use of resources and the most effective service—the major responsibilities that the new manager must grapple with immediately—are treated in the latter half of this chapter. Other requirements of the new job may not be so readily apparent, but they deserve early and thoughtful consideration. Among them are leadership, skill in the development of good interpersonal relationships, and the expert management of self.

LEADERSHIP

The board or governing committee expects from the manager firm control over the library's operations; the staff expects guidance in the performance of its duties. Neither group may be able to define managerial leadership in more precise terms or to name the attributes of the person they think likely to be successful in practice. In fact, the potential for leadership may reside in many persons and is probably not dependent on any given set of traits. Successful leadership grows from an intricate matrix whose elements are the characteristics of the leader, the needs and attributes of the followers, the goals and structure of the organization, and the social, economic, and political climate in which leader and led function.

By thoughtfulness and example, the new library manager can lead the staff to successful performance of the library's mission. Some guides to good leadership conduct are offered by E. F. Wells:

"A great leader is approachable but not familiar, courteous but not weak, decisive but not dogmatic, understanding but not gullible, receptive to new ideas and suggestions but not too easily influenced. His rules are essential, not frivolous, and they are applied fairly. When things go wrong, he accepts the responsibility for his workers, but when they go right, he gives them credit. He is himself an example to emulate, most of his excellent results are due simply to his own outstanding performance."

The manager by example can set the pace of work and standard of performance for the staff—a powerful way of teaching: as Albert Schweitzer stated so forcefully: "Example is not the main thing in influencing others. It is the only thing."[1]

INTERPERSONAL RELATIONSHIPS

The new manager, whether moving up in a familiar organization or moving into a new one, will quickly be aware of standing in a changed relationship to the staff, the board, and the community.

---

(1) Wells, E. F., **What An Executive Should Know About the Fear of Leadership.** (Chicago: Dartnel Corp., 1977), p. 5.

While remaining as friendly as ever with the staff, the new manager must exercise great care to be objective and fair with staff members as individuals. Each staff member will rightfully expect equal support and encouragement and equally consistent treatment. There should be no favoritism. It cannot be overstressed that success in managing a staff depends on cultivating the kind of objectivity that is both real and apparent.

Success in other relationships demands the same objectivity. With a board of trustees or directorial committee, the new manager has not just one boss, as formerly, but many. While being sensitive to their individual values and diverse ways of interpreting their responsibilities, he or she must be objective in interpreting their joint directives. Although the board and the manager are likely to share the responsibility for policy decisions, the board will expect the manager to present recommendations for formal approval and to draft language for such statements. It is expected that these will be based on a dispassionate view of what is best for the library.

The new manager also steps into a different role in the community served by the library. This means new or changed relationships with community leaders, other agency heads, or other department heads in the parent organization. Because the library administration makes decisions that affect these people and the library users who also come under their concern, the library manager must cultivate harmonious working arrangements with them. This should include taking the initiative in consulting with them about the needs of their clientele who are also library users (Sinclair 1979). It is particularly incumbent upon the new school librarian to establish quickly good rapport with the students and sound working relationships with the principal and the teachers.

MANAGING ONESELF

Working late hours and habitually carrying work home mark an ineffective person and one whose energy reserves will be soon depleted. A good manager makes time for home life, recreation, and the enrichment and perspective provided by experiences that are quite outside the job (Brown 1973).

A poor apportionment of workday time, whether because a manager is self-centered, overcommitted, or disorganized, results in great inconvenience to others. The manager who fails to keep appointments, or who comes to them late or unprepared, wastes the time of everyone with whom he or she does business.

A daily plan—and the wise person will schedule every hour—will not only conserve time but even seem to stretch that valuable commodity. Allotting the first fifteen minutes of each day to planning the day's activities and deciding which few items must be accomplished without fail will reduce the number of crises and ensure that commitments will be met.

Having established a sense of order and appropriate priorities for one's own day is essential, for the manager can then be calm and unrushed in dealing with the questions, problems, and interruptions that are both inevitable and impossible to schedule. The manager needs to be able to move smoothly from one concern to the next, dealing with each as expeditiously as possible, since delays in solving problems or providing needed information can cause serious frustrations to the staff and aggravate any problems that may already be lying beneath the surface.

The day's schedule should permit the manager to be sufficiently available to attend to important questions and to return urgent telephone calls. For example, it is better to allow an hour between two meetings than to schedule them back-to-back. Flexibility is important and should be built into the schedule.

Delegation of management tasks wherever possible is another effective way to win extra time, and it can also provide other benefits. For one thing, there is a better chance that all the jobs that should be done will get done and on time. For another, interesting and challenging managerial tasks can be shared with the staff, providing excellent training for the middle managers who may be required to act for the manager in the latter's absence. Still another benefit is that the planning and coordinating expertise which is (or should be) the manager's strong suit will be fully exercised by delegating tasks for others to perform.

PLANNING AND ORGANIZING THE WORK OF THE LIBRARY

During the early weeks of the new job, the manager must give thought and time to planning the library's work for the coming year and organizing the staff to accomplish that work in the best possible way. Usually this means taking over from a predecessor and trying to pick up programs and activities already scheduled. There is little time for formal planning and little possibility of starting things from the beginning right away, but the new manager should review the progress and the rationale for each program. At this point, use of a task force of staff members is a good way to review and evaluate the library's programs, not only because the staff is the best source of information but also because the manager will develop team spirit and commitment to the programs by involving staff in the evaluation and the future planning.

Periodically throughout the year there should be evaluative review of library programs. In the case of the public library, public acceptance and support should be determined from written evaluations of programs by attendees, from requests for materials and services not provided currently, and from any complaints by users. If community needs have not been assessed within two years, the library should make such an assessment to provide information for future planning (Palmour and Bellasai 1980). Collecting and analyzing the necessary information takes a great deal of time and effort, which cannot be supplied by staff alone; help must be enlisted from Friends of the Library or a local planning commission.

In the case of special libraries, a similar evaluation would include consultation with heads of departments, researchers, and frequent users; and the circulation of questionnaires designed to reveal special user needs and areas for collection building.

Evaluation and planning for a school library media center, of which the program must be integrated with curriculum planning, would involve the director's attendance at all staff curriculum sessions, early and frequent conferences with the principal, and continuous consultation with teachers. The school librarian can ask the district supervisor to evaluate the library media center and find out how well it measures up to that of other schools and to established guidelines and standards. Both students and teachers can be questioned as to how well the center meets their needs.

In addition to program planning, the new manager will be required to devote time to budget, salary, and staff development planning. The budget is very probably determined a year in advance, but the new manager should understand how it was arrived at and how much is budgeted for each area of major expenditure: salaries, materials, utilities and rent, supplies, equipment, and other costs. A review of expenditures from the current year's budget to date is mandatory, so that a determination of the rate of spending and the adequacy of the budget to cover the year's costs can be made. The manager should consult the board of trustees or other policy making authority concerning its role in the budget planning process and approval of expenditures. Fiscal management and accountability of funds are key functions of the library manager that should receive attention very early after assuming the new job. The staff should be involved in planning the budget, so that they understand the library's fiscal position and the need for establishing priorities.

ORGANIZING

In many special, school, and very small public libraries, the manager is the only employee and must provide all services, perform all housekeeping tasks, and represent the library to management or the community. This situation offers challenge and freedom, but it can also be lonely and frustrating. A professional librarian who accepts such a position is often unprepared for the clerical and routine tasks that must be done if good service is to be offered.

In other small libraries the staff is so small (two to four people) that each member has specific duties that are already well established when the new manager arrives. There may be little that it is possible to change in the way of work assignments, but it is wise to review the job content, establish the continued necessity of each task, and ensure that the best methods are being used. The staff should participate in the review and any changes that may result. These libraries often require that the manager be involved in providing public services to supplement the staff.

When the small library has a staff of five to fifteen people, the new manager should study the present organization of functions and the qualifications and placement of the staff, then identify changes needed to strengthen the library's ability to deliver quality services. Actual changes or reorganization may not be made for several months, but the review and assessment of strengths and weaknesses should begin early in the new job. When reorganization does occur, the staff members affected should be involved in the planning and decision making if the changes are to be accepted and supported.

FORMAL COMMUNICATIONS

The new library manager will find that there are requirements for formal communications that will be different from those of the former job. There will be written reports to the board of trustees and local officials, the school principal, or upper level management in the case of special libraries. There also will be many oral and written communications to the staff in the form of staff meetings, counseling sessions, and memoranda. These could require as much as 25 percent of the manager's time, since each one must be researched and prepared in advance. The library manager should also strive to build a reputation for well-documented and interesting presentations to community and professional library groups.

INTERLIBRARY RELATIONS

In this age of cooperation and resource-sharing among libraries of all types, it is important for the new library manager to learn what arrangements exist with respect to reciprocal borrowing and photocopy privileges. It may be necessary to establish relationships with other school, college, public, and special libraries, if none have previously been formed.

If the new manager has come from another community or state, he or she should investigate the availability of local library associations and multitype cooperatives, the importance the board attaches to them, and the role the staff and former manager have played in them, so that these relationships can be continued. Such initiatives on the part of the new manager signify willingness to carry a fair share of responsibility for the successful cooperation of local libraries. All libraries—large and small—have a great deal to contribute to such ventures.

BIBLIOGRAPHY

Brown, Geoff. "Finding Time to Manage." *Management Review* 62 (September 1973): 47-49.

The best managers know how to plan their work and keep time-wasters to a minimum. If a manager is working long hours and spending a large amount of time fighting fires, he/she should keep a diary for a month to find out just where the time is going, which jobs should have been delegated, what problems are not being solved, and where poor communications have caused interruptions and delays.

Palmour, Vernon E. and Bellasai, M. *A Planning Process for Public Libraries.* Chicago: American Library Association, 1980.

A new approach to standards for library service based on local community conditions and needs. Planning consists of determining needs, strategies to reach standards, and continous monitoring of progress with adjustments as conditions change.

Shaughnessy, Thomas W. "Library Administration in Support of Emerging Service Patterns." *Library Trends* 28 (2) (Fall 1979): 139-149.

Services and programs are ways libraries cope with their environment. Changing service requirements and the application of technology in libraries demand adjustments to organizational structure such as decentralized decision making changes in staff attitudes and behaviors, and increasing staff specialization and departmentalization. These changes require library administrators to spend more time coordinating functions, redesigning jobs, evaluating services, and assuring that funds are allocated for optimum benefits.

Sinclair, Dorothy. *Administration of the Small Public Library.* 2d ed. Chicago: American Library Association, 1979.

The roles of the library and the library director in the community are essential to success: meeting community needs for information, working harmoniously with the board, and setting standards for quality services. This book provides very useful information to the new, inexperiences library manager on how to do a community study, the role of the board and the purposes of policies, personnel administration, finances, interlibrary cooperation, and the management of buildings and equipment.

4

COMMUNICATING WITH THE STAFF

Staff morale, performance, and productivity; staff absences and turnover: it is these factors which largely decide whether a library functions well or ill, economically or wastefully. Good communication between the manager and the staff can turn them from negative to positive to the library's benefit.

In a small library the manager, the supervisors, and the staff members often work in close proximity. In any case, they communicate constantly, by memo, telephone, talk, gestures, tone of voice, and even posture. The free flow of information that is so necessary to the smooth functioning of the library can only take place in an atmosphere of friendliness and mutual trust in which staff members speak without hesitation and supervisors really listen (Lorey 1976). Many managers do not realize that they are figures inspiring awe and sometimes even fear in the staff. They must try to be sensitive to feelings and aware of undercurrents.

The manager should express appreciation of ideas offered by staff members; should take their problems seriously and assist with their attempts to find solutions. If staff ideas and suggestions are implemented, credit should be given where it is due. If staff members' suggestions are not used they should be given the reasons. Neglecting to do the latter is a frequent and bad mistake.

The manager who treats staff concerns lightly or gives the impression that staff problems are inconsequential will soon stop hearing about these concerns and problems and will have deprived himself of a powerful managerial tool. The administrator who establishes open communication with staff will gain invaluable knowledge of the staff members' strengths and weaknesses, their individual dependability in the daily run, and their likely reactions to crises and unforeseeable demands (Lorey 1976). The manager's concern and support also serve to alleviate the stress experienced by some workers who must deal with the public day in and day out.

THE ART OF LISTENING

Staff members deserve the manager's undivided attention when they come to discuss matters of concern to them. By not seeming to be too busy or about to rush off to another appointment, by adopting a relaxed manner, and, above all, by actively listening, a manager can encourage a worker to be open, to "get things off his chest", to think his message through. The active listener, besides paying close attention to what a speaker says, will also strive to recognize the thoughts and feelings that may lie beneath the spoken words. This skill can be improved with practice.

The nonlistener, concentrating on what he himself is going to say next, effectively destroys communication. So does the interrupter who rushes in on another's unfinished sentence with "I know what you mean, but . . ." Such a person will never have the benefit of the other's thoughts and is likely to stop discussion altogether. Nonlisteners are inconsiderate and insensitive; library managers cannot afford to be among them.

BARRIERS TO COMMUNICATION

It cannot be said too strongly that the chief barrier to communication is nonlistening, but there are other hurdles, including fear and even the very words used to communicate (Schachat and Anastasi 1979).

Everyone uses language in the context of his experience, with the result that two people using the same words may be expressing very different thoughts. A staff worker who refers to "a good department head" may mean someone who is interested in people, does not shun responsibility, and inspires his or her staff by hard work and example. A manager using the same phrase may mean someone who gets the job done within budget and schedule, looks for cost-saving methods, and stretches the staff to the limit in order to achieve increasingly difficult goals. A librarian may use the term "on-line services" to mean a list of references to books and articles that may not be available in the library at all, whereas the patron envisions a product delivered into his hands at the press of a button.

Fear, more often a factor in the work environment than most managers and supervisors realize, is a barrier to communication. It may be the result of uncertainty, lack of information, feelings of inadequacy, the attitude of a supervisor, past experiences of punishment or reprimand, or anticipation of failure or ridicule. Managers should be careful to criticize actions but not persons. They should never poke fun at a staff member or indulge in cruel teasing. When correcting errors, they should be careful not to make a staff person feel stupid or ridiculous (Tracy 1979). Corrections should be meted out in private.

The staff will keep problems hidden from supervisors who communicate by reprimand. The supervisor who approaches a problem by exploding, "Mary, you've got to learn to file properly!" will subsequently have to work with a resentful and frightened Mary whose filing is not likely to be improved by her feelings of failure and inadequacy. The episode will possibly have all but shut the door on future communication with Mary on any subject.

A more thoughtful supervisor can initiate a dialogue that is much more likely to arrive at the desired result:

> Supervisor: Mary, someone seems to have misfiled material in the first drawer of the vertical file. When you have time, will you put it in order?
>
> Mary: Yes, I'll do it first thing this afternoon. I'm afraid I haven't explained the system carefully to Peter, who sometimes files in the evenings. And I think some of our patrons have been refiling material; they don't seem to notice the sign about leaving material in the basket. I wish we could think of a better system.
>
> Supervisor: Will you bring the question up at the next staff meeting? Maybe we can get some ideas from the rest of the staff.

Whatever Mary's failure may have been, whether in filing or in supervisory oversight, she is more likely to correct the problem in a positive way, and the communication door has not been shut.

THE TROUBLED EMPLOYEE

No library staff can be free of illness, personal problems, and job- and home-related stress or worry. From time to time the supervisor will be required to deal with employees who are troubled and unable to perform at their best. What are the symptoms of such problems? The supervisor who has come to know each staff member will notice behavior changes such as preoccupation, fatigue, irritability, absences, changes in disposition, and a deterioration in performance and productivity.

What can the supervisor do to help? Very often a staff member simply needs to air a trouble, and the sensitive supervisor who can take time just to listen will take care of many problems. Recognizing changes in mood and performance and asking whether the staff member is bothered by something is often the only invitation to talk that is needed.

More serious problems, such as physical illness or emotional disturbances, family crises or alcoholism, require professional help and should be referred to medical or other specialists for treatment (Menninger and Levison 1956).

THE MANAGER SETS THE TONE

The library manager, more than anyone else, determines the effectiveness of communication within the library by setting an example and determining policy (Baird 1979). In addition to mastering the art of intelligent, sympathetic listening, the library manager must devote a considerable part of every day to hearing what staff members have to say. This means taking time to talk with them, individually and face to face. In these exchanges the manager should seek to discover how each staff member thinks and feels and should leave each person with the feeling that he or she is important to the manager and to the work of the library (McCaskey 1979).

How can the manager establish pleasant, effective communication with a staff member? **Not** by the peremptory summons to the manager's office, which may thoughtlessly break in on the staff member's work and also fill him with dread. The manager should call to consult the worker's convenience and give some indication of the matter to be discussed; then the staff member, instead of feeling resentful or apprehensive, can come to the conference prepared and comfortably ready for discussion. Neither should the discussion be initiated by an unannounced visit to the worker's desk or station (except for a friendly or interested word in passing), but again in this case, by pre-arrangement of time and topic. Even short notice will be perceived by the staff person as courteous conduct on the part of the manager, and the willingness of the manager to come to the worker as evidence that both are equally important individuals with respect to the work at hand.

WHAT SHOULD BE SHARED?

What information should the manager share with the staff? When? How? The best rule is "everything possible;" "promptly;" "frankly and fully." Some things (such as a personal matter involving an individual employee or difficulties with an individual board member or local official) must be kept confidential. Sometimes a manager may be constrained by his board or executive committee from divulging information prematurely. These considerations aside, there are very few instances when the manager cannot inform the staff (Carter 1974).

The staff need full information with which to make their own job decisions; it is far better to give them too much than too little. Even when the manager tells them more than they need to know to do their immediate jobs, they gain insight into the total library operation and a feeling of belonging and responsibility to the organization. In their personal lives people want to know what is going on around them, and the same is true of their working lives (Hargreaves 1976).

"Everything possible" includes the finances of the library, the problems, and the criticisms of collections and services, along with all the good things that happen. With respect to bad news, it is far better to share it with the staff fully and openly than to have rumors flying around and morale in jeopardy. The manager who is not open, who deals in guarded truths, will erode his or her credibility very quickly; the one who shares information fully and promptly will have a staff that is willing to understand and accept those occasions when they cannot be told or can be told very little.

It is important that the staff get communications from the manager, not from someone outside the organization. If there is a matter that concerns the public, the staff should be told first, if possible; otherwise there should be a simultaneous announcement to the staff and the community.

STAFF MEETINGS

Staff meetings are excellent vehicles for imparting facts about the library's business or reinforcing information already distributed by memoranda and otherwise. Meetings of the supervisory staff are traditional in most libraries and essential for solving problems and exchanging information at the upper levels, but they should be supplemented by open meetings for all staff.

Staff meetings can be invaluable for eliciting staff interest and participation in the work of the library, or they can be a costly waste of time. The library manager who wishes to make the most of them should:

- Schedule them regularly for a given hour and day
- Start and end them on time
- Allow time for staff to mingle and talk with one another
- Encourage discussion.

Above all, the manager should prepare an agenda for the meeting and stick to it. Staff members should be invited to contribute to it, and it should be distributed before the meeting in a form that leaves room for participants' notes. Some libraries have a staff committee to prepare the agenda.

Staff meetings that are open to all employees let each one know that he or she is as important to the operation of the library as anyone else. They also provide the opportunity for manager and fellow workers to listen as individuals deliver committee reports or talk about conferences they have attended. Sharing information promotes camaraderie among the staff and often avoids serious errors in decision making.

POLICY AND PROCEDURES

Organizations must have operating policies and procedures that apply to all the staff. In libraries these range from service policies such as intellectual freedom to rules concerning tardiness. The staff must know what is expected of them and how infractions will be treated. It is part of the supervisor's job to inform the staff and enforce the rules, if the library is to operate smoothly. For example, work schedules should be posted well in advance so the staff can plan free time. When it is necessary for someone to be absent, the person should know what arrangements must be made in advance.

Even the smallest library would be well advised to maintain a procedures manual in which policies and operating guidelines are available for consultation. Clearly written guidelines that are applied equally and fairly to all employees help eliminate employee complaints and dissatisfaction.

WRITTEN COMMUNICATIONS AND NEWSLETTERS

The library manager should send a written communication whenever a staff member will need it for future reference, whenever it is necessary that all staff receive identical information, or whenever all staff should be notified quickly. Examples of matters requiring written communication to staff are job opening announcements, changes in policy, and emergency notices (Emery 1975).

A newsletter, if issued regularly and on time, is an effective way to describe job openings, recognize individual or committee work, and announce social events. Feature articles, with pictures of staff members, are a great boost to morale and provide a kind of recognition that is very important to some workers. Newsletters are often staff produced with space allotted to the director.

BIBLIOGRAPHY

Baird, John E., Jr., and Wieting, Gretchen K. "Nonverbal Communication Can Be a Motivational Tool." *Personnel Journal* 58 (September 1979): 607-610.

Expectations of superiors and managers influence the behavior of employees. The behavior of the boss, rather than what he/she says, is critical to the communication of expectations.

Carter, E. A. "My Communication Philosphy? It's Full Disclosure." *Industry Week* 183 (October 21, 1974): 50-52.

An electronics company uses employee meetings, a newsletter that answers complaint questions, and open management meetings that include employees' spouses as ways to improve communication and create an environment of openness.

Emery, Richard. *Staff Communication in Libraries.* Hamden, CT: Linnet Books, 1975.

Some barriers to communication are organizational structure, physical working conditions, language, personalities and attitudes, and a stressful environment. Presents a plan for improving communications. Various forms of communication, both oral and written, are discussed.

Hargreaves, John. "Six Keys to Good Communication." *International Management* 31 (December 1976): 54-56.

The what, why, when, how, where, and who of communications are discussed. Emphasis is placed on keeping employees informed, so that they feel they know what is going on and are free to ask for more information. Timely and accurate information provides employees with insight into the relationship of their work to the work of others, gives them a sense of belonging, and improves their sense of status and importance in the organization.

Lorey, Will. "Mutual Trust is the Key to Open Communications." *Administrative Management* 37 (September 1976): 70-92.

Decision making based on full communication between employees and management is best. Employees feel they are trusted members of a team when they are included, but frustrated when they are left out.

Caskey, Michael B. "The Hidden Messages Managers Send." *Harvard Business Review* 57 (November-December 1979): 135-148.

Managers' body language, place of communications and use of imagery carry—and often are—messages. Communications involve sentiments and feelings; they can be disrupted when persons involved use different meanings for words or employ joking and put-downs. Physical settings are important to communications; managers who are sensitive to place as territory will let the purpose of a meeting determine where it will be held. Body language, tone of voice and pacing convey messages that may not be intended by the words used. Eye-to-eye contact is a very powerful communication tool; managers should keep eye contact when listening to others.

Menninger, William C. and Levinson, H. *Human Understanding in Industry...A Guide for Supervisors*. Science Research Associates, 1956.

A handbook of source materials for human relations training in industry. Good discussion of personality, how it is molded, and its effect in the work place.

Schachat, Robert and Anastasi, Joel. "Face-to-face Communication: Breaking down the Barriers." *Supervisory Management* 24 (April 1979): 8-14.

Cites poor communication skills of managers and supervisors as a major contribution to poor morale, high absenteeism and turnover, and low productivity among employees. Describes the barriers of fear, failure to listen, defensive behavior and other impediments to communication.

Tracey, William R. "Put-down Techniques: Are You Guilty of Them?" *Personnel Journal* 58 (May 1979): 311-313.

Describes put-down techniques that some managers use, such as the peremptory summons, inattentiveness, public reprimand, and abrupt treatment of subordinates. Describes the effect on employees and gives rules for overcoming the most commonly used put-downs.

5

THE MANAGER AS SUPERVISOR

When the manager of a small library is the only professional on the staff, he or she must spend some time supervising the work of others. Most of the general management advice given in the two preceding and two following chapters applies equally to the situation of the manager-supervisor, but with important differences in respect to scheduling, delegation of duties, staff development, and personal relations.

Self-management and scheduling of the manager's own time are more critical, for those who must manage as well as supervise, for the manager-supervisor must perform additional different tasks: planning and scheduling the work of individual staff members, making sure that their work is done efficiently and cost-effectively, assuring that their equipment and facilities are kept in good working condition, and assessing individual performance. Although managing a small, nonprofessional staff may require greater self-discipline, it can also give the satisfaction of seeing the goals of the library accomplished very directly through the manager's own good supervision and ability to maximize his own professionalism.

DELEGATION OF WORK

How does one achieve a balance among all of the activities necessary to both manage the library and supervise others? The answer lies largely in delegation of work and, to the extent possible, of authority also. The librarian who tries to shoulder the major part of the work, as well as the responsibility of the library, is almost certain to fail as the library's manager.

Delegation of work is imperative when there is more to be done in the normal work week than the director can manage, and when there are routine tasks that another person could do. It is important also that there be trained and trustworthy staff members who can fill in for the librarian during scheduled or unforeseeable absences.

What should not be delegated? Matters of importance that only the director should handle and those that the director is best equipped to deal with because of special expertise or knowledge; problems; and tasks that involve confidentiality (Bittel 1968).

Successful delegation is dependent on the manager's informing the employee of:

- The scope of the job or the specific result to be achieved
- The importance of the job and why it has been delegated
- What authority he has and how far he can go in making changes that affect others
- Any time limitations or deadlines
- How, when, and to whom to report
- How much supervision and follow-up he can expect from the manager and at what point.

If delegation of a task to one staff member affects the work of others, they should be informed that he has been given the job to do and what his authority limits are. Other workers must understand their roles so that all can work together harmoniously.

Delegation will fail if the staff are unable or unwilling to do the work. If there are not qualified people to undertake the jobs that should be delegated, the delegation process will be slow at best; nevertheless, there will be small tasks, errands, and filing on which to begin. As time passes, the new manager may have opportunities to select new staff who are better qualified through education and experience to handle more difficult assignments.

GIVING DIRECTIONS

New managers who have been accustomed in past positions to taking, rather than giving, instructions may need guidance as to how to give directions. Suggestions include the following:

- Be full, clear, and specific in making an assignment of work
- Repeat instructions, if necessary, to be sure they are understood
- Describe the expected results, but avoid dictating how the work is to be done
- Encourage the staff member to think the task through, ask questions, and decide for himself how to do it
- Do not withdraw a job or make changes in it, then inform the staff member later
- Do not ask a staff member to do something as a favor when a directive is meant.

PERSONAL RELATIONS AND COMMUNICATIONS

The manager-supervisor—more visible and in more frequent contact with the staff than in libraries where other supervisors intervene—must be careful in interacting with the staff to avoid creating the apprehension that a worker is likely to feel in dealing with the chief.

Of necessity the manager-supervisor must monitor the work of individuals, which will include appearing unannounced at various work areas. A reassuring approach and a display of consideration for the worker will ease such encounters. A few words such as, "Don't let me interrupt you; I just need to look up something here," or "I just thought of something I'd like your advice on; but don't change your lunch plans—it can wait till later," will build rapport.

Some staff members may be reluctant to approach the director with their work and personal problems. Scheduling report or conference times with each staff member will obviate this difficulty.

When situations arise that require changes in the way things have been done in the past, the staff cannot be expected to know, and may be totally unaware, of the need for change. At the same time, they need to be told that improvements or corrective actions are required and what their role is to be. The manager or supervisor must provide the facts, outline how the new system or procedure is to work, and which staff members will be involved in the change. As described in Chapter 4, open and full communications are often all that is needed to provide the direction and achieve the results desired.

MOTIVATING THE STAFF

Studies of workers from many occupational levels have shown that interesting work and authority to get the job done are ranked ahead of pay and security as important in their jobs. They want to be kept informed, to be able to communicate their ideas to management, and to contribute to the organization (Sinetar 1980).

All staff members are different: they come from various backgrounds, families, and schools; their lifestyles, values, personal and professional standards and goals will vary. Supervisors who know employees' backgrounds can understand the needs their jobs can help satisfy and make job assignments that motivate good performance.

Supervisors who strive to provide an environment that meets the expectations of employees must exhibit behaviors that support such a climate: provide recognition of the work, treat everyone fairly and impartially, respect each individual, permit freedom of expression of opinions and ideas, be concerned for each as a person, provide sympathetic help on personal problems, be tactful in disciplining, and provide opportunities for advancement. The supervisor will try to understand the perspective and viewpoint of the staff and how they feel about their work; will be consistent and predictable in temperament; and will be enthusiastic about the library and its accomplishments (Bittel 1968). The good manager-supervisor projects an image of the library's potential for service, beyond what it has yet achieved.

When the staff fail to perform, or make mistakes, the good supervisor will look for the reasons: do they know how to do the job? Is it busywork that is really not needed? Is it dirty work that seems unfair? Is there a fear of failure and reprimand? Mistakes that are treated as learning experiences encourage the staff to find ways to solve problems or try new ways. The supervisor who treats mistakes as catastrophes and metes out penalties will build an atmosphere of fear, anxiety, or resentment.

The good supervisor will request actions rather than give commands, make suggestions rather than rules, and show appreciation rather than take efforts for granted. He or she will get the facts before making a judgment, and the staff will feel at ease and will look forward to coming to work.

BIBILIOGRAPHY

Bittel, Lester R. *What Every Supervisor Should Know.* New York: McGraw-Hill Book Co., 2nd Edition, 1968.

Comprehensive coverage of the first-line supervisor's job including which techniques work and which do not.

Josefowitz, N. "Management Men and Women: Closed vs. Open Doors." *Harvard Business Review* 58 (September-October 1980): 56.

A study of men and women managers: women tend to be more accessible to subordinates, whereas men devote their time to their career pursuits. Men focus on operations and planning, using their time to work undisturbed; women are more likely to have their doors open to interruptions by their staff. Accessibility has a positive aspect in that it fosters rapport with the staff, contributes to their satisfaction and growth, and improves the quality of life for both manager and managed.

Menninger, William C. and Levinson, H. *Human Understanding in Industry...A Guide for Supervisors.* Chicago: Science Research Associates, 1956.

A handbook of source materials for human relations training in industry. Good discussion of personality, how it is molded, and its effect in the work place.

Sinetar, Marsha. "Management in the New Age: An Exploration of Changing Work Values." *Personnel Journal* 59 (September 1980): 749-755.

Reference in Chapter 1 (which see).

6

STAFF DEVELOPMENT

Staff development—which may encompass anything from training in the use of a computer terminal, through a workshop on interlibrary lending, to post-graduate courses in community relations (for the public library) or in building a research collection (for the special library) or learning to integrate media with curricular areas (for the school library)—should be part of every library management plan and every library budget. Rapid change makes it increasingly essential.

Staff development is an investment in the human resources of the library. It is important to the continued viability of the organization in that it builds the key resource, which is the staff. Libraries cannot afford to lose ground in the information-oriented world in which they must function by failing to keep pace with the new technology and new knowledge. At the same time they must recognize the intrinsic needs of the staff for job satisfaction on the one hand and for personal growth on the other. The library manager who considers staff development a time and money consuming luxury should think again. The library really cannot afford **not** to invest in staff development as a long-range and continuous activity, for human performance problems can prevent attainment of library goals. Training and development programs designed to resolve problems can bring about changes in staff attitudes, skills, and knowledge that will result in more effective and economical functioning (Warren 1969). Haphazard and undirected training is not apt to be fruitful, however, nor is it likely to be satisfying to the staff. Staff development should be included in the total library plan for the year and as carefully budgeted for time and money as other library programs (Kaser 1971). A development scheme for each individual staff member should be part of his or her program for the year.

Some clues to the need for training in various areas will arise from complaints, crises, requests, suggestions, and staff grievances. Some will grow out of the appraisal process discussed in the following chapter. At the annual performance appraisal, and at less formal conferences as the occasions arise, the worker and his or her supervisor will uncover areas where special training or education will result in better job performance, greater self-satisfaction and ultimate advancement for the staff member. Some staff will be eager for development opportunities and will seek them; others will need administrative encouragement and support—even prodding if the library's interests are at stake.

Development should not be limited to those in top positions or to the formal concept of continuing education defined in terms of academic courses, professional meetings, workshops and seminars. Most of these take place outside the library and entail a cost in fees and staff time that many small libraries cannot afford. The library manager who takes a broader and more imaginative view might draw up a list of staff development opportunities that would include the following possibilities:

- On-the-job training
- Coaching on a one-to-one basis
- Providing feedback on performance
- Listening and counseling
- Reading
- Self-instruction
- Job exchange or rotation within the library
- Job exchange with other libraries
- Training as back-up to other staff members
- Mentor relationships between experienced and new staff members
- Committee membership, e.g., summer reading program or National Library Week programs
- Attendance at city council meetings

- Presentations about the library to other community organizations
- Membership on interorganizational committees in the community
- Book talks to the institutionalized users
- Writing for publication
- Consulting on library studies
- Visiting other libraries to observe their practices
- Teaching in library science programs
- Formal academic programs to earn degrees
- Refresher courses
- Seminars
- Workshops
- Meetings and conferences
- Research.

All of these are possible in some libraries and some of them are possible in all libraries, no matter how small the library or the staff. It should be noted, however, that some of the above activities should not be undertaken by inexperienced staff members. They should be given prior training and the opportunity to observe capable performance by others before being expected to assume such responsibilities as giving book talks or serving on outside committees.

DEVELOPMENT OF ADMINISTRATIVE PERSONNEL

Staff librarians who are promoted to supervisory positions (and the observation is equally applicable to the new library manager) may tend to carry upward with them tasks better delegated to individuals who report to them. Part of their development should be focused on learning to turn over such work and also a significant portion of the decision making concerning it. Development plans to be initiated at the time of promotion will result in stronger supervisors and more capable and enthusiastic workers reporting to them.

Mace (1950), in describing the development of executives, says, "The objective of the executive's job, in other words the coach's job, is to utilize the abilities and capacities of others. Effective utilization means developing the latent potential of subordinates. Coaching subordinates is, therefore, not some technique to be adopted and used by administrators as a tool, a method or a device. It is a way of administration; it is administration."

Three kinds of managers can be categorized according to their effectiveness, the least effective being those who do their subordinates' work for them, rather than teaching them how to do it and then leaving them alone.

To a second group belong those managers who do their own jobs well, but expect others, including their subordinates, to teach themselves without the benefit of coaching. They are sometimes effective managers, but they run the risk of costly problems and staff discontent.

The most effective managers not only do their own work well; they know the elements of good performance in all of the jobs in the enterprise and are ready and willing to provide the coaching that subordinates need.

At the time of performance appraisal an employee and his or her supervisor can pinpoint areas where the worker might improve on-the-job performance if given specialized training, and a development plan can be written to allow for such training in the ensuing year. An astute supervisor will, however, be alert to the possibility of developing a staff member in areas outside the narrow confines of his present job to provide greater flexibility and back-up for the library and career enhancement for the individual. For example, if a circulation assistant has demonstrated proficiency at operating an on-line circulation control system and is interested in other mechanized operations, he or she might be trained to become a reference assistant who performs literature searches using on-line search techniques and services.

The alert supervisor should also be on the lookout for staff members who would benefit from a change of jobs or the opportunity to learn to do the same job in new ways. The steady performer who has been in the same job for a long time may or may not wish for a different assignment. Some people in this situation tend to become highly specialized and resist any change at all, preferring to remain in jobs from which promotional opportunities are rare. They may, however, welcome training workshops and other aids to learning better ways to do their work.

MODEL STAFF DEVELOPMENT PLAN

An example of a development plan for a public library with nine staff members is given below. The library contains 15,000 volumes and serves a population of 10,000. It belongs to a 20-member multicounty library cooperative. The staff consists of a director; the supervisor of public and adult services, who is also the reference librarian; the supervisor of children's and young adult services; two circulation assistants; one reference assistant; one assistant for children's programs, a secretary and a bookkeeper. The following figure shows the reporting hierarchy.

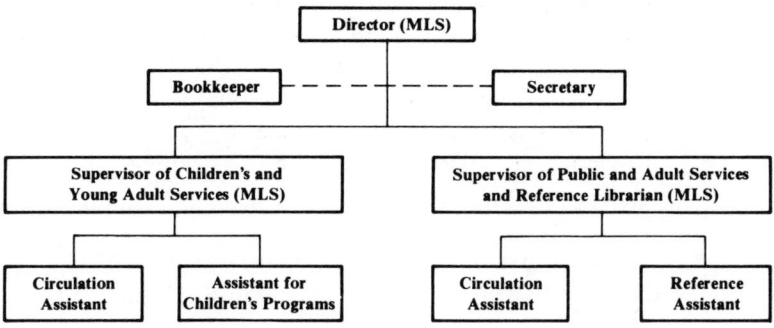

At a meeting in early January, an all-staff discussion is held to draft library objectives for the year for discussion and approval by the Trustees. Individual staff development plans to meet the objectives must be determined. The director, who is new to the job, has learned that a community information needs analysis has not been done for five years. During this period the town has grown by 2,000 residents and has acquired two new industries and a new community college, so there have been significant changes in expectation and demands for the library. It is agreed that a survey should be undertaken in the spring and that, in the meantime, reference services and interlibrary loan should be strengthened and improved to meet the increased demands for information that the library is already receiving from students and local businesses. In the course of the year, the library expects to acquire the benefits of an automated circulation system through its participation in the multicounty cooperative, so the library's circulation assistants must be trained in its use. These tentative plans agreed upon, pending the results of the community analysis, supervisors and staff prepare individual development plans in conjunction with the director of the cooperative.

I. Development Plans for Non-Professional Staff

  A. Circulation Assistants' Training Objective: To learn to operate the computerized circulation system.

   The two circulation assistants will be trained to operate the new system by participating in sessions held at the headquarters library of the Cooperative. They will spend four half-days working in the circulation department and receiving instruction from the supervisor in charge. Upon completion of this training, they and their supervisor will receive instruction from the trainer of the Computer Circulation Co., who will spend two half-days at the site. The circulation assistants will subsequently teach the system to their reference assistant, who with this training will be able to serve as a back-up.

  B. Reference Assistant's Training Objective: To learn to conduct effective interviews and do question analysis.

   The supervisor of public services will provide coaching to the reference assistant on interviewing users. Great skill is often required to analyze a question, to determine its real meaning and to recognize when it is necessary to refer it and the inquirer to the supervisor. A review of actual questions and the responses supplied provides valuable opportunity for feedback and improvement of techniques. A slide-tape instructional package on reference interviews and question negotiation will be rented for use by the reference staff and others who may be working with the public, e.g., the circulation assistants. This package can also be used for reference training in special libraries.

C. Assistant for Children's Programs' Training Objective: To learn to tell stories.

The supervisor of children's and young adult services will provide training to the assistant to prepare her as a back-up. This will be done through coaching and demonstration. The assistant also will visit the headquarters library story hours to observe different storytellers, and to view films that are available and listen to master storytellers on recordings.

D. Secretary's Training Objective: To serve as contact with other secretaries in the Cooperative and to assist in the processing of interlibrary loan requests.

The secretary will visit the Cooperative headquarters library and other secretaries to become acquainted with the resources and to establish good working relationships. She will assist in processing interlibrary loan requests by verifying references.

E. Bookkeeper's Training Objective: to become knowledgeable of computer applications to bookkeeping.

The bookkeeper will attend a state library workshop on computer applications in libraries.

II. Development Plans for Professional Staff

A. Supervisor of Public and Adult Services' Training Objective: To improve the quality of reference service and to implement the computerized circulation system.

The supervisor will spend one afternoon a week for six weeks at the headquarters library working in the reference section to assess the role of the local library as a participant in the overall reference services of the cooperative. This will provide an opportunity to use a larger reference collection and to recognize how the head quarters staff can serve as a resource. Also, **nonlibrary** information and referral resources in the area should be identified and some communication and/or relationship with them established, if possible. At the least, the system headquarters and all local member libraries should know what other resources are operating (800 numbers, "hot lines", etc.) and be aware of their scope, and the particular needs to which they are geared.

The supervisor will then be in a better position to provide the coaching to the reference assistants as outlined previously.

The supervisor will provide coaching to the circulation assistants on the mechanized circulation system, being alert to problems as they arise and consulting with the Computer Circulation Co. as required.

The supervisor will attend one workshop on reference services sponsored by the Cooperative and one seminar on management of small libraries at the State Library. It will be important also to keep abreast of the current literature on reference and circulation services.

B. Supervisor of Children's and Young Adult Services' Training Objective: To improve the quality of services through planned collection building with the public school libraries.

The supervisor, who is new to the library, will review the programs and evaluate the collection for children and young adults. He/she will visit the public school librarians, working through the District Director of Library Media Programs to develop cooperative activities for sharing resources.

After attending a seminar sponsored by the State Library Association on services to young adults, the supervisor will develop a plan to expand services to this group. The library has not had a formal program for young adults in the past.

C. Director's Training Objective: To determine community needs for library and information services and to identify areas of cooperation with other agencies.

The director will work with the newly formed Friends of the Library to plan for the needs assessment and analysis. According to the timeline, the data collection phase will begin in six months. In the meantime, the director will visit other service agencies, attend city council meetings, and accept invitations to speak to community groups. He/she will consult with the Board of Trustees concerning the library's past role in the community and elicit their ideas and approval about its proposed future role.

III. Costs/Time Requirements

The costs for the staff development program should be estimated and included in the plan. They include direct money outlays in the form of fees and travel expenses and such indirect costs as staff time. The costs for the foregoing plan would be as follows:

A. Fees and Travel Costs
   Seminar fee of $50 — State Library Association
   Travel and lodging costs — $100 $150

B. Tape Rental $ 75

C. Staff Time (off-site)   176 hours
   Supervisor of Public Services
      Seminar — 8 hours
      Workshop — 8 hours
      Headquarters in-service — 24 hours   40 hours
   Supervisor of Children's and Young Adult Services
      Seminar — 8 hours   8 hours
   Circulation Assistants
      Headquarters in-service
         4 days @ 8   32 hours

On site training	
2 days @ 8	16 hours
Reference Assistant	
To cover circulation desk (back-up)	
2 days @ 8	16 hours
Training for inter-library loan	
4 days @ 4	16 hours
Reference Assistant	
In-service tape slide program	
2 days @ 4	8 hours
Children's Assistant	
To cover circulation desk (back-up)	
2 days @ 8	16 hours
Headquarters to observe story hours	
2 days @ 4	8 hours
Secretary	
Visit to headquarters and three other libraries	
4 days @ 4	16 hours
Bookkeeper	
Workshop	8 hours

BIBLIOGRAPHY

"ALA Guidelines to the Development of Human Resources in Libraries: Rationale, Policies, Programs, and Recommendations." *Library Trends* 20 (July 1971): 97-117.

Development programs and activities such as courses, orientation programs and in service training, are not the total means for developing the library's human resources; and environment which permits and encourages individuals to develop their potential is required. The individual and the organization share the responsibility for development through professional commitment by the one and awareness of organizational need for viable staff by the other. The chief administrator must take a leadership role in establishing policy for staff development and in allocating funding to provide an adequate financial base.

Conroy, Barbara. *Staff Development and Continuing Education Programs for Library Personnel: Guidelines and Criteria.* Boulder, CO: Western Interstate Commission for Higher Education, 1974.

> Fifteen guidelines and supporting criteria are provided that cover planning, implementing, and evaluating programs. In some sections suggestions are offered for meeting the guidelines.

Kaser, David. "The Training Subsystem." *Library Trends* 20 (July 1971): 71-77.

> Few libraries are doing anything to provide staff development in any organizaed way, as evidenced by the fact that so few hava a budget line item to cover such costs. Steps for development of a training program are given: state the need to be satisfied, define objectives that will contribute to satisfaction, define the organization constraints, generate alternatives, select the best alternative, implement it, evaluate results, and modify the program on the basis of the evaluation. Advocates the coordination of all continuing education opportunities into a single, library-wide subsystem that is planned for and budgeted like other parts of the operation.

Mace, Wyles L. *The Growth and Development of Executives.* Boston: Division of Research, Graduate School of Business Administration, Harvard University, 1950.

> It is possible to reduce costs in organizations by developing the skills and capacities of the people who work in them. In spite of management's agreement to this principle, it often neglects this phase of operations. There is no item in the profit and loss statement that directly reflects the cost of inadequate attention to the development of people. The symptoms of neglect are bad morale, high turnover, and absenteeism.

Martell, Charles R. and Dougherty, Richard M. "The Role of Continuing Education and Training in Human Resource Development: An Administrator's View point." *Journal of Academic Librarianship* 4 (July 1978): 151-155.

Continuing education, whether formal education or on-the-job training, is an important way for staff to achieve personal growth. Other benefits are a strengthening of library services and programs and improvements in the quality of work life. Some employees view it as a fringe benefit that enhances their career opportunities.

Musmann, Klaus. "Socio-Technical Theory and Job Design in Libraries." *College & Research Libraries* 39 (January 1978): 20-28.

Socio-technical theory considers organizations to be purposive and the individuals within organizations to be purposive, whole human beings who shape society by interacting with technology to satisfy their own needs and those of the organization. The application of these concepts tends to develop satisfaction yet efficiency in job performance. Job design in libraries should consider the goals of the individuals and those of the library, and provide for career movement as programs change and individuals develop.

Odiorne, George S. *Training by Objectives.* New York: Macmillan Co., 1970.

An objective for training/development is the specification of the desired level of skill or end result. Training should not be used out of zeal, interest, or as an attempt to cure symptoms of a problem. Without an objective there is no problem, and training is not needed.

Porter, Lyman W.; Lawler, Edward E.; and Hackman, J. Richard. *Behavior in Organizations.* New York: McGraw-Hill Book Co., 1975.

People are a unique organizational resource which often prove difficult to develop, maintain, and utilize. They have their own career objectives that may or may not fit the organization's plans. The development of people increases their value to the organization and to future employers. People want to utilize their skills and abilities, and if they cannot, may leave an organization.

Stone, Elizabeth W. "Personal Development and Continuing Education in Libraries; Introduction." *Library Trends* 20 (July 1971): 3-18.

Societal changes are causing libraries and the people who work in them to attach a new importance to personnel development and continuing education. A dual emphasis is needed: on meeting technological changes, and addressing individual needs for personal as well as professional development.

Warren, Malcolm W. *Training for Results*. Reading, MA: Addison-Wesley Publishing Co., 1969.

Organizations continue to waste, misuse, and exploit their human resources. Training can be a good tool if managers and supervisors focus on problem solving and development and move training from the classroom or seminar back to the job. The results of training must be changes—in skill, attitudes and knowledge—that benefit the organization and the individual.

Weber, David C. "The Dynamics of the Library Environment for Professional Staff Growth." *College & Research Libraries* 35 (July 1974): 259-267.

Individuals accept jobs for more than salary reasons: pride in the work, identification with the organization and its goals, opportunity to work with respected people and to achieve personal growth and advancement. Staff development is the most important factor in a satisfactory long-term personnel program and is fostered by a conducive work environment.

7

PERFORMANCE APPRAISAL

Performance appraisal is the process of evaluating an employee's contribution to forwarding the work of the library and meeting library goals. There is debate over the value of performance appraisal (McGregor 1957) and a good deal of discussion of the problems that can arise if supervisors are inept in its administration. Such appraisals can be worthless and even detrimental if personal traits rather than performance of a worker are emphasized. If, however, the process is formalized and the worker shares in the process, benefits can accrue to both employee and library. Employees learn how well they are doing their jobs and what is expected of them if they are to earn pay increases and promotions. Managers can pinpoint job-related problems and areas where employees need training and development and can identify the need for additional staff with new and different skills (Carroll and Tosi 1977).

INFORMAL APPRAISALS

In most small libraries appraisal is based on the judgment of the director and the supervisors. If a rating scale is used, it is likely to be based on work-related and personal characteristics: work quality and quantity, cooperativeness, reliability, and so forth. The supervisor does the rating by checking an appropriate box on a simple rating form that will probably not be differentiated by anything more than the designations of good, fair, needs improvement, or poor. The individual may not be consulted, involved, or asked for self evaluation.

In another informal method the supervisor keeps a record of incidents of positive and negative job behavior and performance. On the positive side go such entries as successful organization of a story hour or patron praise for good service; on the negative, tardiness or poor telephone etiquette. The strength of this method is in the record of specific cases that can form the basis for discussion between supervisor and staff member and substantiate the overall rating for the period.

A third appraisal method is often used by libraries to evaluate clerical operations in cataloging, acquisitions, and circulation. The supervisor sets standards for each task, instructs the employee as to what they are, and judges the employee's performance on the basis of achievement.

Each of these methods has the shortcoming that there is usually evaluation by the supervisor only, without involvement of the staff member. It is not always clear to the individual being evaluated just what the basis of evaluation will be or how it relates to his or her development and growth. For this reason it is recommended that small libraries adopt a planning approach to performance appraisal based on the setting of objectives and involving the supervisor and the staff member in a partnership of planning and problem solving that is positive and considerate of individual needs and sensitivities.

It is also important that libraries improve their performance appraisals because of the increase in the use of evaluations by the civil service and because appraisals are necessary to complete the evaluation components of federal grant applications and awards.

MANAGEMENT BY OBJECTIVES

Performance appraisal that relies on a formal process of reviewing and evaluating employee performance rather than on a supervisor's memory, expectations, and subjective judgment is not new, having been practiced by industrial managers for at least a hundred years. Concept and use have, however, undergone change.

Merit rating, in vogue fifty years ago, employed a standardized rating form for worker evaluation. It was popular with administrators but not with unions, who preferred seniority as the criterion for promotions, wage increases, and retention in the face of layoffs. Employees in non-unionized companies also preferred seniority as the basis of administrative actions concerning personnel.

In the 1950s, Peter Drucker introduced a concept which he called "management by objectives" (MBO) that has been adopted by many organizational planners. Simply stated, an MBO plan sets individual objectives necessary to achieve group objectives, and group objectives that contribute to organizational ones. Because an individual's work progress and achievement is measured against his objectives, performance appraisal is a necessary part of MBO.

Top management support and full employee participation are essential if MBO is to work, and both supervisors and staff need a period of practice in its use. When these conditions are met, MBO can be very effective in small libraries.

LIBRARY APPLICATION OF MBO

The manager's first step is to form a task force of staff members to discuss the library's goals for the year, and identify some objectives for achievement of those goals. The objectives should be stated in measurable terms. For example, one objective aligned with others under the goal of "reaching out to new groups of potential users" might relate to initiation of services to the homebound. In measurable terms, one could call for meeting the objective of (1) locating the homebound of the library's community and (2) beginning service to 5 percent of them the first year. The goals, which should be related to the library's mission and based on prior assessment of community needs, form the basis for the general work plan for the year. Each worker can see what the special library objectives are and can tie his or her performance to the strategies for working toward them. Cooperation and good team spirit generally result from an understanding of common purpose.

Department and individual objectives are then set to ensure achievement of the objectives. Taking the example of service to the homebound, the circulation department might be charged with identifying the number and location of persons who would use the service. One staff member might be assigned the task of devising and administering a survey instrument for arriving at usable figures for budgetary purposes; another might plan which 5 percent of the group will constitute the pilot. The success or failure of these staff members in accomplishing the assignment would constitute one item in their performance appraisal.

The next step is a general meeting with supervisors and staff to gain their understanding of the MBO process and the method for applying it. Both staff and supervisors will need to become familiar with the rating forms (Appendix 1, Examples 1 and 2) that all supervisors will use.

Each staff member will then meet with his or her supervisor to develop an individual work plan for the year. The staff member should be able to see the direct relationship of particular tasks to the work of the department and to the library's overall goals and objectives.

Individual objectives are put in writing, and employee and supervisor agree that the degree to which they are accomplished will be the basis of the employee's annual appraisal. Some staff members will need guidance and possibly several years of practice to become comfortable with the process of selecting activities, developing time schedules for achievement, and defining results.

Both the employee and the supervisor keep copies of the plan for referral and together throughout the year monitor progress and work out solutions to problems. Coaching and counseling are required of the supervisor if there are to be no surprises at the time of the annual appraisal. At the end of the plan year the individual is encouraged to complete the self-evaluation portion of the form, and at a subsequent interview supervisor and staff member review this assessment and talk over any points on which they may differ (Hitt 1979). This interview is probably the most difficult part of the evaluation process for both participants, and many supervisors may not have the skills to handle it well. Enabling training in the conduct of interviews may have to be included in supervisors' own development plans. As McGregor (1957) has said: "Personnel administrators are aware that appraisal programs tend to run into resistance from the managers who are expected to administer them. Even managers who admit the necessity of such programs frequently balk at the process—especially the interview part." Supervisors who do not want to be responsible for permanently damaging the career of an employee by making performance appraisal part of a written record that is used to determine salary, promotions or lay-off may be too kind in both the interview and the written appraisal.

The interview is a prime time to establish positive communication between supervisor and staff member (see Chapter 4), and the MBO approach to performance appraisal is a boon to supervisors who might otherwise feel uncomfortable in talking to an employee about his performance. When performance is measured against agreed-upon objectives, staff shortcomings can be discussed in terms of further training and development and preparation for promotion that may follow upon greater endeavor. The kind of negative and destructive criticism that can make some workers defensive and leave them emotionally crippled for weeks or months is less likely to be employed by the supervisor.

Development and training objectives are incorporated into the staff member's work plan for the ensuing year, and the appraisal cycle recommences.

VALUE OF PERFORMANCE APPRAISAL

The positive method of performance appraisal that focuses on the joint efforts of supervisor and staff member to set performance objectives and evaluation standards should:

- Provide the staff member with a clear understanding of his job responsibilities

- Establish mutually agreed upon objectives for the staff member with a commitment of support and problem-solving assistance from the supervisor

- Establish performance standards and a time schedule for the staff member that are challenging but reasonable and achievable

- Provide for periodic reviews of progress so that problems are identified and solved as they occur, and before a buildup or backlog develops

- Assist the staff member in identifying his potential, recognizing opportunities as they are presented, and adjusting to personal limitations

- Have a stimulating effect on the staff as they learn that their abilities and efforts are appreciated

- Eliminate informal and random evaluations based on the supervisor's memory or subjective judgment

- Identify training and development needs of the staff member and encourage him to take the initiative to acquire new skills and knowledge.

Performance appraisal that is a year-long coaching and feedback process can have a positive effect on a staff member. When a supervisor as helper pools his or her experience and knowledge with the ideas and energies of the worker, the employee feels valued as a person and a staff member. He is assured of help with his problems and comfortable about offering ideas and suggestions to his superiors. Although the joint problem-solving approach to improved performance requires a greater commitment of time and energy on the part of supervisors than the ad hoc method in which the supervisor serves as judge, it pays far greater dividends in the long run, for people and for libraries.

BIBLIOGRAPHY

Brandwein, Larry. "Developing a Service Rating Program." *Library Journal* 100 (February 1, 1975): 267-269.

Union, management, and employees of the Brooklyn Public Library cooperated to develop new promotion policies and a new evaluation form designed to rate job performance, personal characteristics and supervisory ability, with space for comments by two raters and the employee. The Library subsequently developed a Service Rating Manual to explain the form to supervisors and staff members. The rating form is included in the article, and the manual is available from the Library.

Carroll, Stephen J. and Tosi, Henry L. *Organizational Behavior*, pp. 286-295. Chicago: St. Clair Press, 1977.

Describes methods of performance evaluation, sources of error such as rating leniency and bias, conducting the review, and ways to improve results obtained from performance review, such as converting criticism into specific improvement goals.

Hilton, Robert C. "Performance Evaluation of Library Personnel." *Special Libraries* 69 (November 1978): 429-434.

The literatures of both general and library management are reviewed and discussed. A management-by-objectives approach to performance evaluation is recommended, together with day-to-day coaching by supervisors to aid in problem solving and staff development.

Hitt, William D. "This is Synergy: A Model for Humanistic Educational Management." *NASSP Bulletin* 63 (May 1979): 7-15.

Humanistic management combines the principles of management by objectives and participative management to achieve high productivity for the organization and fulfillment for the employees. The manager carries out such activities as providing a helping relationship, communicating, motivating, problem solving, decision making, innovating, and team building. Staff participate as team members to perform tasks; they are taught to assess needs, develop objectives, and prepare plans. The individual evaluates his own performance.

McGregor, Douglas. "An Uneasy Feeling About Performance Appraisal." *Harvard Business Review* 35 (1957): 89-94.

Discusses the author's concern about performance appraisal that requires the manager to pass judgment on the personal worth of subordinates; instead proposes a system that gives the subordinate primary responsibility for establishing performance goals and appraising progress toward them.

Mollenhoff, David V. "How to Measure Work by Professionals." *Management Review* 68 (November 1979): 39-43.

A state government agency employing professionals (researchers, consultants, accountants, and social workers) whose performance had been difficult to measure instituted management by objectives. Performance indicators—called "key result areas"—were devised to provide measurable standards. Methods are described and examples given.

Morano, Richard A. "An Rx for Performance Appraisals." *Personnel Journal* 58 (May 1979): 306-7, 328.

Recommends a performance appraisal system based on criterion referenced measurement (e. g., preestablished performance objectives for individual workers) rather than a norm-referenced system that compares the performance of one person with that of others in the group. Also recommends that pay be linked to performance and rewards given to superior performers.

8

COMPENSATION

If they are to offer good service, libraries must attract and keep well-qualified staff. To do so, they must pay their staffs adequately. It is important for the library manager to understand the issues affecting library salaries, how the value of a job to the organization is established, and the need for salary planning. This chapter addresses those matters.

ISSUES

Librarianship historically has been a predominately female profession and is likely to continue to be, as women currently constitute 80 percent of library school graduates receiving the MLS degree (Slanker 1976). School librarians, who are certified professionals, but not always holders of the MLS degree, are 92 percent women. The result has been lower salaries for all workers in the field, men as well as women having been paid less than workers in other professions for jobs requiring comparable education and experience (Galloway and Archuleta 1978).

The assumption that a lesser value may be assigned to jobs traditionally held by women than to those held by men is being challenged by the library profession. Librarians in San Francisco, San Diego, and Montgomery County, Maryland, are formally appealing for equitable salaries. The Maryland librarians have brought the issue to the attention of the U.S. Equal Employment Opportunity Commission, which has admitted that the Equal Pay Act and even the concept of equal pay for equal work do not fully address the problem (Leach 1979). The San Francisco Bay Area Chapter of Women Library Workers has made a study which shows the inequities they suffer as a result of sex discrimination; it recommends changes in the job classification system and the city charter to provide that library salaries be based on comparable worth rather than on the present system of prevailing library wage. Librarians at San Diego Public Library have filed suit in federal court challenging the inequity between salaries of librarians and salaries of other city employees with comparable jobs (Galloway and Archuleta 1978).

In general, female librarians are paid lower salaries than male librarians, especially for administrative and top management jobs (Heim and Kacena 1979). This is true of academic, public, and special librarians alike, as revealed by a recent Special Libraries Association survey that showed female SLA members receiving lower salaries than male members when the number of persons supervised or the years of experience were equal (Hoban 1979). With school librarians, however, there is no pay differential between the sexes, since their pay scale is the same as for teachers, with rate of pay based on credentials and experience.

A third compensation issue is whether rates of pay for library specialists should approximate those for library administrators, on the premise that both may make equally important contributions to the work of the organization. A pay plan based on this assumption presents dual career paths to professional recognition and financial reward rather than only the traditional one up the administrative ladder (Weber and Kass 1978). Although this is less likely in the small library, it is definitely important in one that is large enough to employ specialists.

WAGE FACTORS

Like any other organization, a library must establish its rates of pay. Some of the determining factors are external to library control: the cost of living, the library's or the parent organization's budgetary circumstances, and the availability of qualified workers. Probably the most important external determinant is the pay offered by other area libraries. Assuming other conditions of employment are reasonably equal, staff will become dissatisfied if their rates of pay fall measurably below those offered by other libraries of the same size. It is recommended, therefore, that library managers stay informed of salaries and wages paid by other libraries and strive to pay as well as they do.

Two factors that affect staff pay are determined internally by the library director or the personnel board. The first is job classification, which is discussed in the following section. The other is differentiation between two workers whose job descriptions or work responsibilities are the same or much alike; here the manager and the personnel advisor must discriminate on the basis of individual experience, skill, education, performance, and attitude. In the public sector, promotion may be the only possible way to recognize and reward superior performance, whereas special libraries in the private sector can use salary increases for this purpose.

Figure 1 shows some of the conflicting pressures on a library's wage levels. All of the pressures are not present all of the time; for example, if the economy is in a downturn, rates of turnover in response to wage levels usually decrease rather than rise. School libraries are not affected by wage level pressures to the same extent as other libraries—unless schools are closed—for two reasons: most of them are staffed by certified professionals whose salaries are established by the district; and they tend to use volunteers to augment the staff. When rising costs drive wages up, there will be an increase in the hiring of nonprofessionals for professional jobs, particularly in special libraries. In fact, many private sector organizations see no need to hire professionals for their libraries at anytime. In some smaller public libraries also, the director may not be a graduate librarian or even a college graduate in another field. The practice of hiring nonprofessionals often relates to the going wage rate.

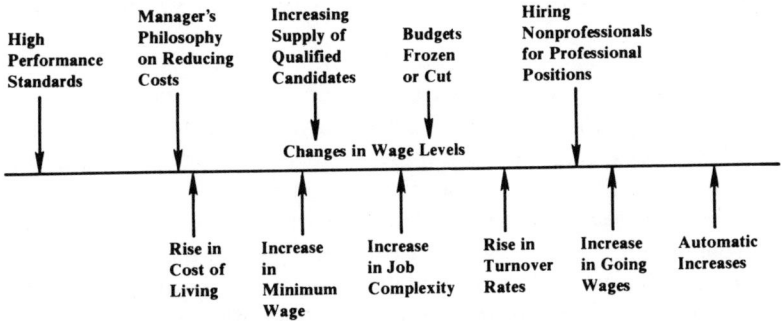

FIGURE 1. WAGE LEVEL PRESSURES

JOB EVALUATION SYSTEMS

A library may use one of several job evaluation systems for establishing the worth of a job to the organization and translating that value into pay.

The simple ranking of jobs according to their value to the library is a method employed by many small libraries. It is done by listing all jobs, then assigning a rank number to each, starting with the two that are the highest and lowest in value, then ranking the remainder, starting with the second most important and proceeding downwards. Figure 2 illustrates the procedure. This informal method of ranking tends to be based largely on the manager's subjective judgments, and it is often done without the benefit of good job descriptions (Berg 1976).

Jobs	Ranking
Cataloging clerk-typist	5
Janitor	8
Circulation clerk	6
Senior clerk, acquisitions	3
Computer terminal input operator	2
Secretary	1
Page	10
Reference assistant	4
Mail clerk	7
Copy machine operator	9

FIGURE 2. RANKING OF NONPROFESSIONAL POSITIONS

A more formal evaluation system is based on skill levels. Examples are the civil service classifications used by federal, state, and local governments that apply to most government and public libraries. In these systems a predetermined number of grades are established, each grade being ranked on the general characteristics of the jobs it encompasses. For example, jobs in the lowest grades would carry very little latitude for the exercise of independent judgment, whereas workers in the middle grades would have some opportunity to make unsupervised decisions, and staff in higher grades would be expected to make independent work-related decisions.

A professionally supplied service called a point plan is more widely used in industry and the private sector than in the public sector and is more likely to be employed by special than by general libraries. In this system for evaluating jobs and determining pay, factors are established for each job, points are assigned to the factors, and the rate of pay for the job is determined by the number of total points assigned to it.

There are two widely known point plans in use today: the Hay System and a system developed by the National Metal Trades Association (NMTA). The NMTA system uses factors such as education, experience, supervision received, working conditions, and complexity of duties. It is best applied to non-professional positions. The Hay System correlates factors such as requisite knowledge and skills, the incumbent's freedom to apply his knowledge and skills without supervision, and the extent to which he is accountable for the management of fiscal and other resources. The Hay System is most often applied to top positions and tends to favor line over staff jobs. This discourages assigning comparable compensation to technical and administrative positions (Berg 1976).

The job classification schemes generally used in libraries cannot usually indicate a differential for outstanding performance, which will tend to discourage the high achiever from putting forth continued effort to do a superior job. Automatic pay increases, which may largely be for cost-of-living rises, may not be viewed as sufficient reward by this worker. Although one may nowadays read in the management literature that pay does not motivate the worker whose prime need is for self-realization (Desatnick 1976; Sinetar 1980), most workers consider the pay they receive to be recognition of the most substantial kind, especially if they feel it is related to performance (Piamonte 1979).

JOB DESCRIPTIONS

A good job description should state the factors which determine the value of the job and be the basis for the pay associated with it. It should include the following:

- Job title

- Statement of the primary area of responsibility (e.g., managing the cataloging department)

- Objective of the job as it relates to the mission of the library (e.g., the cataloging department staff will process all new acquisitions within two weeks of receipt to maintain currency of the collection)

- List of major duties

- Qualifications required.

Since the job description determines pay and is the basis for judging performance, it is important to the staff member's morale and motivation that it be open to him (Berg 1976). When changes in library programs or services necessitate reevaluation of a job, the incumbent should be invited to participate in rewriting the job description. He will construe the invitation as an expression of trust in his judgment and be more likely to find the resultant changes acceptable.

SALARY PLANNING

Library managers expend up to 75 percent of their budgets on salaries and wages, an expenditure that must be well managed if it is to purchase in a competitive market the kind of staff that is required in the present technological environment. A yearly salary plan should be submitted with the annual budget to the library's board even though the city personnel office establishes pay rates. This information gives the board the necessary facts to defend the budget. The plan should include the following:

- Current market value of each job

- Salary range for each job including minimum, midpoint, and maximum salaries, and the intermediate steps of each grade

- Rules for application of salary schedules

- Guidelines for determining salary increases (flat cost-of-living adjustments; automatic increases based on time in grade; required study for movement in grade and salary, if any; merit increases,etc.)
- Amount budgeted for salaries including increases for the next year
- Amount currently spent on salaries
- Proposed increases with effective dates for staff members receiving them. Those not scheduled for increases should be listed.

Many organizations use an employee task force to do the salary planning. This method improves communications with the staff in the important area of pay determination; it also acquaints them with the economic facts of the organization. A third significant advantage is that their input and ideas produce a more realistic plan and one that is acceptable to them (Nash and Carroll 1975).

Today's average library staff members, more highly educated and sophisticated than their counterparts of even a decade ago, are often as well equipped to deal with the library's economic problems and the sensitivities of pay as their managers. The salary planning task force can grapple with the thorny problems of market value of jobs, inflation rates, budget cuts and program cut-backs, and their recommendations are likely to be of considerable value to the manager and the board. Task-force membership is a valuable developmental experience for staff members—some will find this kind of involvement satisfies their higher order needs for self-fulfillment. It also provides an opportunity to the library director to assess individual capabilities for solving problems and taking on future management jobs. The appointment of a task force indicates to the staff a trust in them which builds morale and team spirit.

BIBLIOGRAPHY

Beacham, Samuel T. "Managing Compensation and Performance Appraisal under the Age Act." *Management Review* (January 1979) : 51-54.

To avoid discrimination charges organizations need to abandon job evaluation systems that use highly subjective judgments such as ranking and point factor plans. A better way is to use a statistical technique that identifies the variables that explain compensation differences; e.g., number of employees supervised, number of levels down from the chief executive officer, staff versus line positions, years of education, length of service and time in position. Major flaws of most performance appraisal systems are vagueness of performance standards used, too much subjectivity and inconsistency among appraisers, and inconsistent application of results from supervisor to supervisor. A sound system is based on the measurement of observable, job-related criteria; is standardized in its application across the organization, and can be shown to be nondiscriminatory.

Berg, J. G. *Managing Compensation.* New York: Amacom, 1976.

A treatise on compensation covering the design of wage and compensation systems: the elements, the structure, and the decisions which must be made. The compensation manager's job and the ways in which he can assist in the decision process are discussed.

Desatnick, Robert L. *Innovative Human Resource Mangement* New York: American Management Association, 1976.

Poor human resource management is the primary cause of underachievement by employees, and a majority of executive failures result from ineffective interpersonal relationships. The key concerns of managers are recruitment, development, utilization, compensation, activation, and retention of human resources. Individuals consider challenge, opportunity, responsibility and money, in that order, important to their jobs. Recognition, the work itself and growth are other important satisfiers. The organization and its management must provide the environment, climate, opportunity, and supervision that encourage and foster development of employees.

Fleuter, Douglas L. "A Different Approach to Merit Increases." *Personnel Journal* 58 (April 1979): 225-226.

The primary objectives of a sound wage and salary program are to attract and retain qualified employees. Merit increases based on a percent of the employee's grade midpoint rather than a percent of base salary is recommended. This allows high performers to advance more quickly.

Galloway, Sue and Archuleta, Alyce. "Sex and Salary: Equal Pay for Comparable Work." *American Libraries* 9 (May 1978): 281-284.

Since librarianship is a female-dominated profession, neither men nor women library workers receive pay comparable to that of workers in male-dominated professions. This article describes the actions of librarians in San Francisco and San Diego to gain more equitable salaries through appeals to city government and through lawsuits.

Gambill, Ted R. "A Market-oriented Approach to Salary Administration." *S.A.M. Advanced Management Journal* 14 (Summer 1979): 41-46.

Salaries should be competitive, equitable, and related to performance. Outstanding performance should be rewarded with higher salaries to show recognition and appreciation of achievement. Each salary grade level has a minimum and maximum salary limit reflecting the economic value of the job in the marketplace and recognizing the spectrum of performance differences. It is stressed that pay systems are most effective when tied to results-oriented performance appraisal systems.

Heim, Kathleen M. and Kacena, Carolyn. "Sex, Salaries, and Library Support." *Library Journal* 104 (March 15, 1979): 675-680.

An analysis of relationships between the sex of library directors, their salaries and per capita support in large public libraries. It was found that public libraries with male directors received better support than those with female directors; female directors received lower pay; and salaries are lower for entry-level librarians under a female director than under a male.

Hoban, Mary F., Griffin, Richard E., Baum, Fred, and Andrews, Catherine. "SLA Salary Survey." *Special Libraries* 70 (December 1979): 559-589.

The average salary of SLA members on April 1, 1979, was $19,300, up 18 percent over 1976. The median salary was $18,000, up 20 percent. Salaries are not keeping pace with the consumer price index. In every percentile rank salaries for female members are less than those for male members even when the number of persons supervised and years of experience are equal. Yet the gap does not seem to be closing, since the median female salary was 82 perent of that for males in 1979 as opposed to 81 percent in 1976. Federal government employees earn the highest salaries and library workers in the Washington, D.C., area have the highest median salaries. A ranking by primary responsibility shows library school faculty with the highest median salaries; administrators rank second. Librarians employed in information centers report higher salaries than those employed in libraries. Tables and charts are provided by geographic area, type of institution, and area of responsibility. The survey instrument is included.

Leach, Daniel E. "Federal Policies on EEO in Compensation." In *American Compensation Association 1978 National Conference Proceedings,* pp. 55-57. Scottsdale, AZ: The Association, 1979.

Discusses the EEO Commission's decisions in cases of wage discrimination against women under Title VII of the Civil Rights Act, in which female job classifications are undervalued and underpaid in comparison with largely male job classifications.

Nash, A. N. and Carroll, S. J., Jr. *The Management of Compensation.* Monterey, CA: Brooks/Cole Publishing Co., 1975.

Provides a comprehensive treatment of compensation problems and methods of administration, including legal considerations, employee motivation, determining wage levels, and establishing the value of jobs and their associated pay.

Piamonte, John S. "In Praise of Monetary Motivation." *Personnel Journal* 58 (September 1979): 597-599.

Money is an important incentive if it is related to performance, with excellent performers receiving significantly higher salaries than average performers. Merit pay systems fail because the portion of a pay increase for merit is often very small and is tacked onto the annual cost of living increase. Merit pay in the form of bonuses is recommended if that system is used.

Rock, Milton. "Salary Administration; Past, Present and Future." In *American Compensation Association, 1978 National Conference Proceedings*. Scottsdale, AZ: The Association, 1979.

In the past salary administration played a key role in helping organizations achieve their objectives of attracting, retaining, and motivating high-caliber people. Money should not be treated as a market transaction with employees, but as a reward for achieving certain results and as recognition for achievement. Predictions for the future of salary administration include increased government regulations and requirements, including wage and price controls, increased inflation, and an increased percent of the organization's revenues going for compensation.

Sinetar, M. "Management in the New Age: An Explanation of Changing Work Values." *Personnel Journal* 59 (September 1980): 749-755.

Reference in Chapter 1 (which see).

SLA 1980 Salary Survey Update. *Special Libraries*. 71 (December 1980): 541-542.

This survey reports an overall median salary increase of $1,700 from $18,000 in 1979 to $19,000 in 1980, which is a 9.4 percent increase.

Slanker, Barbara. *Degrees and Certificates Awarded by U.S. Library Education Programs 1973-1976*. Chicago: American Library Association, 1976.

Report on surveys of U.S. library education programs covering number and types of degrees, ethnic background and sex of recipients. Results of three annual surveys are reported and compared.

Weber, David C. and Kass, Tina. "The Case for Equal Compensation for Nonadministrative Expertise...Comparable Rewards." *Library Journal* 103 (April 15, 1978): 824-827.

Discusses the need for administrative specialists in libraries, such as subject specialists with unique academic backgrounds and experience, and points out that these individuals require appropriate rewards. In the past library compensation practices have been based on administrative responsibilities. Advocates salaries based on professional contribution.

Yen-Ran Yeh, Thomas. "Library Peer Evaluation for Promotion and Merit Increase: How It Works." *College & Research Libraries* 34 (July 1973): 270-274.

Library staff at Central Washington State College (7,000 students) have faculty status; all have master's or doctoral degrees. Each one fills out a professional service record with his/her latest achievements in working effectiveness, scholarship, productivity, and professional activities. These records were attached to evaluation forms and served as the basis of peer evaluation by the Personnel Committee, which evaluated each person and recommended promotion or special merit increases. The recommendations were provided to the Dean, who defended each case. Peer evaluation strengthened the Dean's recommendations and the library staff received the highest number of promotions among all departments in the 1971-72 academic year.

9

EQUAL EMPLOYMENT OPPORTUNITY AND AFFIRMATIVE ACTION

Libraries along with other employers are subject to the laws of the federal government concerning equal employment opportunity (EEO), and the laws of their own states and local jurisdictions that prohibit discrimination in employment. The issue is complicated by the number of applicable laws and executive orders, and the numerous agencies assigned responsibility for enforcement of the laws. This chapter attempts to clarify the complexity of EEO by briefly summarizing the laws and suggesting actions library managers can take to ensure compliance with them.

EEO AND AFFIRMATIVE ACTION DEFINED

The terms "EEO" and "affirmative action" are frequently used interchangeably, but the emphasis of each is different. Equal employment opportunity laws, which prohibit discrimination in employment based on race, color, religion, sex, national origin, age and handicap, are intended to ensure that individuals have equal chances in all areas of employment on the basis of their qualifications. The EEO laws apply to recruiting, hiring, training, promotion, job assignment, benefits, discipline, and discharge.

Affirmative action goes beyond EEO and the concept of nondiscrimination in employment by requiring employers to make an extra effort to hire and promote members of the groups protected by the laws and executive orders: minorities, women, the handicapped, and those between the ages of 40 and 65 years (Miniter 1978).

Equal employment opportunity was one of five major issues of the civil rights movement of the 1950's and 1960's; the others were equal education, voting rights, fair housing and public accommodation. The laws and executive orders that apply have evolved and changed over nearly two decades, and it is probable that there will be further changes as the laws are interpreted by the courts.

EEO LAWS

There are no fewer than six major federal laws dealing with equal employment opportunity as well as differing state laws and local ordinances. There are numerous federal, state, and local agencies that enforce the laws. There is no central agency of government that provides information on the total requirements of EEO legislation. However, the Office of Library Personnel Resources (OLPR) of the American Library Association has established committees on minority recruitment and EEO. Library managers can contact OLPR for information and assistance with EEO matters and affirmative action planning (Dickinson 1979). The state library agency of each state is also a source of information on federal, state and local requirements of the EEO legislation.

The first major laws concerning discrimination in employment were written in the early 1960's. The Civil Rights Act of 1964 and the Equal Employment Opportunity Commission that it created were among the federal government's first efforts to achieve fair employment practices on a national scale. Federal legislation and the major provisions of each law are given below (Higgins 1976).

- **Title VII of the Civil Rights Act of 1964** as amended by the Equal Opportunity Act of 1972 prohibits all discrimination in employment based on race, color, religion, sex or national origin in all employment practices (hiring, firing, promotion, compensation, job classification, and other terms, privileges and conditions of employment), union membership, joint apprenticeship training programs composition, union hiring halls, and employment agency referrals. The Act covers federal, state, and local governments, employers of 15 or more employees, and institutions of higher education. It applies to most libraries.

- **Presidential Executive Orders 11246, 11375, 11141, 11478, and 11758** prohibit discrimination in all conditions of employment and related personnel practices.

— 11246 prohibits discrimination based on race, color, religion, and national origin by federal government contractors and subcontractors including libraries in universities and industry that have federal contracts of $50,000 or more, and requires that they develop an affirmative action program within 120 days after a contract begins.
— 11375 amended 11246 to include sex.
— 11141 prohibits discrimination based on age.
— 11478 prohibits discrimination based on race, color, sex, religion, and national origin by federal government agencies and the U.S. Postal Service.
— 11758 prohibits discrimination based on mental and physical handicaps.

- **Equal Pay Act of 1963** is the earliest piece of federal legislation prohibiting discrimination in employment. It amends the Fair Labor Standards Act (FLSA) of 1938 and applies to those subject to FLSA covering compensation (base pay, raises, overtime, bonuses, and commissions). The FLSA provides that employers may not discriminate on the basis of sex where jobs require equal skills, effort, and responsibility under similar working conditions. It covers employees in executive, administrative, professional, and outside salesforce categories, and employees in most state and local governments, hospitals, and schools. It applies to most libraries.

- **Age Discrimination in Employment Act of 1967** protects workers between the ages of 40 and 65 from discrimination in employment practices, union membership, and employment agency referrals. It applies to employers with 20 or more employees, unions with 25 or more members, employment agencies, and federal, state, and local government subunits. It applies to most libraries.

- **Sections 500 and 503 of the Rehabilitation Act Amendments of 1974.** Section 500 covers federal government employment and Section 503 private employment. Presidential Executive Order 11758, covering mental and physical handicaps, implements this law, which applies to federal government contractors and subcontractors, including libraries in parent organizations that hold U.S. Government contracts. Many universities fall into this category.

- **National Labor Relations Act of 1947** (Taft-Hartley) prohibits discrimination based on color, race, sex, religion, and national origin in labor union representation of all employees and employee rights in relations with union and employer and applies to any employer or union in the private sector engaged in interstate commerce or trade. It applies to libraries that have labor unions.

STATE AND LOCAL LAWS

Most of the state and local laws which prohibit discrimination in employment parallel federal laws. Federal law takes precedence except where state and local laws are more stringent. Library managers should consult with their state library agencies and local governments for clarification about applicable local and state laws.

EEO ENFORCEMENT AGENCIES

The major federal government enforcement agencies for EEO legislation are the Equal Employment Opportunity Commission (EEOC) and the Office of Federal Contracts Compliance Programs (OFCCP). The former can take action against a private employer if a person files a discrimination charge, and the latter monitors affirmative action programs required by law. For actions against discrimination in the federal government, individual agencies enforce the law, with final authority resting in the U.S. Civil Service Commission.

The major federal laws dealing with EEO and the enforcement agencies for each follow:

- **Title VII of the Civil Rights Act of 1964** — EEOC is the enforcement agency for the private sector and government agencies; the U.S. Civil Service Commission is the agency for the federal Government.

- **Presidential Executive Orders**
  - 11246 and 11375 — OFCCP and the contracting federal agencies.
  - 11478 — individual agencies and the U.S. Civil Service Commission.

- **Equal Pay Act** — Wage and Hour Division of the U.S. Department of Labor.

- **Age Discrimination in Employment Act** — Wage and Hour Division of the U.S. Department of Labor for private employers, unions, and employment agencies; and the U.S. Civil Service Commission for the federal government.

- **Rehabilitation Act. Executive Order 11758** — OFCCP and the contracting agencies.

- **National Labor Relations Act** — the National Labor Relations Board. The individual can initiate enforcement agency action by filing a discrimination complaint with the appropriate agency within specified time limits.

FEDERAL REQUIREMENTS FOR AFFIRMATIVE ACTION

Written affirmative action programs are required of federal government contractors and subcontractors by Presidential Executive Orders 11246 and 11375, and OFCCP Order No. 4. These two orders require affirmative action to ensure that employers make extra efforts to hire and promote individuals in the protected classes.

OFCCP Order No. 4, issued by the Office of Federal Contracts Compliance Programs in 1970 and amended in 1971 to include women, contains instructions for the design, implementation, and control of federal government contractor and subcontractor affirmative action programs. Order No. 4 also requires the identification of areas of minority and female underutilization (i.e., areas in which these groups are underrepresented in the work force on the basis of their percentages in the population from which they are recruited), goals for hiring and promoting minorities and women, the assignment of program responsibility, and control of program results.

OFCCP Revised Order No. 14 contains the OFCCP checklists used by federal agencies to audit contractor affirmative action programs.

The EEOC and the OFCCP have published guidelines on the following:

- Discrimination practices related to sex, religion, national origin
- Pre-employment inquiries
- Selection procedures for hiring
- Records and reports required of contractors
- Overall affirmative action program requirements
- Obligations of contractors
- OFCCP audit checklists.

These guidelines should be consulted before designing affirmative act programs.

THE AFFIRMATIVE ACTION PROGRAM (AAP)

A written affirmative action program (sometimes called a plan) is required under Executive Orders 11246 and 11375 and the Rehabilitation Act for federal government contractors and subcontractors that employ 50 or more persons and have contracts of $50,000 or more. An AAP is voluntary for compliance with Title VII of the Civil Rights Act which applies to most libraries. The written AAP must address the following areas for EEO compliance:

(1) Organizational policy for EEO and top management support

(2) Assignment of administrative responsibility for EEO

(3) Analysis of work force to determine how many minorities and women are currently in each job classification and department of the organization

(4) Analysis of work force to determine whether minorities and women are being employed in appropriate numbers in all job classifications based on their percentages in the population from which they are recruited

(5) Numerical hiring and promotion goals, with a timetable for overcoming underutilization of minorities and women where it exists in job groups

(6) An examination of personnel practices currently in use to ensure EEO: recruitment, selection, testing, training, transfers, promotion, layoffs, termination, and others

(7) "Good faith" efforts to achieve goals.

The American Library Association encourages libraries to prepare affirmative action plans and to file them with the ALA Equal Employment Opportunity Subcommittee. ALA policy No. 106.11 prohibits job discrimination in libraries based on color, race, sex, creed, age, physical or mental handicap, individual life style, or national origin. The EEO Subcommittee will review the individual library's affirmative action plans and provide feedback for their improvement (Dickinson 1979).

Written affirmative action plans are a way for library managers to review their current personnel practices for compliance with EEO legislation and to protect themselves and their staffs against discrimination grievances (Mood 1980). Under Title VII of the Civil Rights Act, written plans are voluntary; however, the value of written affirmative action plans cannot be overemphasized. Plans are useful tools to help identify past discrimination practices that need to be corrected, and they familiarize the staff with equal employment opportunity requirements.

PERSONNEL PRACTICES AFFECTED BY THE LAW

The primary practices affected by EEO are recruitment; selection for hiring; selection for transfer, training, promotion, layoff, termination and recall; pay and benefits; and performance reviews. In all of these areas, it is illegal to discriminate on the basis of age, sex, race, color, religion, handicap, and national origin. Library managers and supervisors should be aware of the specific practices in which discrimination can become an issue in these areas (Mitnick 1977).

RECRUITMENT

Applicants for library jobs, as well as employees, are protected by the EEO legislation and the recruitment of new employees must be free of discrimination. Magazine and newspaper advertising, interviewing, and selection must not reflect race, sex, or age biases. For example, an advertisement must not specify "man" or "woman" or make a statement such as "young man wanted".

Library managers need to recruit minorities actively by placing advertisements in minority newspapers, and by contacting state employment agencies, local colleges, and high schools. They must be careful not to set excessive job requirements; specifying a high school education when the job can be done without it could be viewed as discriminatory. Active recruitment is required to change the effects of past discrimination practices, which have resulted in few minority or ethnic group members having been chosen to fill library jobs (Cuesta 1980). Less than five percent of library school degrees are held by such persons, so there is a shortage of them available to fill professional positions; however, it is not sufficient to cite this fact as a reason for not recruiting them.

Depending primarily on referrals from current staff members or other librarians as a recruitment device can result in discrimination since library staffs are predominantly Caucasian and the referrals will be disproportionately white. In this case, the result of the practice, not its intent, is in violation of the law.

Although librarianship has long been a predominantly female profession, women have been discriminated against in their attempts to advance to top management jobs; they are underrepresented in this area with respect to the numbers of women available and qualifed (Schiller 1970). Affirmative action can remedy this situation.

SELECTION FOR HIRING

Selection for hiring usually results from a review of application forms, interviewing of the candidates for specific jobs, and checking of references. All of these practices are affected by the EEO laws, with which library managers must take care to comply if they would avoid discrimination charges.

Federal law does not prohibit asking for information regarding an applicant's race, color, sex, religion or national origin but such questions will be regarded with suspicion by compliance agencies since they are usually irrelevant to job performance. The law is not concerned so much with what is asked but how the information is used. Some state laws, such as Ohio's, do not allow certain questions to be asked either on application forms or in interviews (Ohio Civil Rights Commission 1977). It is unwise to include any question on an application form that aids in identifying the race, sex, age, color, handicap, religion, or national origin of an applicant. Such questions should not be asked of an individual until after hiring. In the case of handicaps, only questions about those that would result in significant hazard in performing the job are permitted.

Other provisions of the EEO laws prohibit questions concerning arrests without convictions, type of discharge from military service, and availability for work on weekends. Minorities tend to have proportionally more of the first, and the last might seem to inquire about the applicant's religion. A discrimination charge could result in either case. Title VII of the Civil Rights Act provides for reasonable accommodations to the religious needs of applicants and employees through scheduling, make-up time, or substituting others whose religions do not forbid their working on Saturday or Sunday. Staff discontent over such arrangements is not a sufficient reason for employers, such as libraries, to refuse to accommodate their staff.

Appendix 2 is a sample application blank that complies with Federal EEO laws.

INTERVIEWS

Interviews of job applicants constitute an important area that is affected by EEO laws. Questions should be limited to those which are job related. A good job description of each position in the library can serve as the basis for questions in the interview. As in the case of application forms, library managers should guard against any questions that help identify the age, religion, race, handicap or national origin of the applicant during the interview. Questions should not be asked concerning an applicant's credit rating or home ownership, or about education and experience not required for job performance. Questions should not be asked of women that are not asked of men; or of minorities that are not asked of nonminorities (Omahan 1978).

Permissible questions might include those about past work experiences and duties, kind of supervision received, and area and level of responsibility; or questions about topics on the application form requiring clarification, such as job changes, periods of unemployment, and absenteeism. It is permissible to ask an applicant about availability to work flexible hours including evenings and weekends, if all applicants are asked the same question (ALA 1972).

The interview is very vulnerable to charges of discrimination, and is likely to come under even closer scrutiny as employers increasingly favor the interview over the use of tests as selection devices (Dipboye 1976).

REFERENCE CHECKS

Library managers who use reference checks as part of the selection process need to be aware of their liability under EEO law. Also they should know that under the Federal Privacy Act of 1974 individuals are entitled to see that their records are accurate and complete. Employers can use the following guidelines to protect themselves when asking for reference checks:

- Ask applicants for permission to check the references given on the application form

- Inform applicants about the types of information to be collected about them before checking the references
- Ask former employers only job-related questions, and preferably present them in writing.

For employers who are requested to provide background information, the following guidelines apply:
- Always get permission of the applicants to release information about them. A copy of the application form provided the prospective employer is usually sufficient.
- Supply only work-related information and only that which is requested. Answer only questions concerning employment dates, attendance records; promotions, salary, and reasons for termination (Omahan 1978).

If an individual is refused a job on the basis of information collected through reference checks, the employer must be able to show that the information indicated that the person could not reasonably be expected to perform the job successfully and that the checking procedure was consistent for all applicants. The burden of proof is on the employer.

SELECTION FOR TRAINING, TRANSFER, LAYOFF, RECALL, PROMOTION AND TERMINATION

The concept of equal employment opportunity requires that women and minorities be given special consideration for training and development that will prepare them for promotion. Transfers and promotions of these groups are coming under increased scrutiny by the EEOC and affirmative action enforcement agencies. Organizations must make special efforts to train and promote women and minorities if they are to be found in compliance with affirmative action legislation.

In the areas of layoff, recall, and termination, employers not only must not discriminate on the basis of sex, age, and race, but also must exercise particular care to document their decisions and actions, especially in the case of terminations. Involuntary termination or discharge of employees is the area in which more discrimination charges are made against employers than any other (Mitnick 1977). An employer should record the disciplinary actions and warnings that precede a dismissal and be sure that the employee receives copies of these records before a discharge is made. Such recording of disciplinary actions tends to reduce the number of discrimination grievances and is well worth the time required.

PAY AND BENEFITS

The Equal Pay Act requires that employers provide equal pay and benefits for equal work to both men and women, minorities and nonminorities.

In the field of librarianship there is the issue of equal pay for comparable work. It is a sex-segregated occupation that underpays both men and women. This unresolved issue is receiving the attention of the library profession. The crux of the matter is that library workers in a traditionally female occupation receive lower pay compared to workers in traditionally male occupations although the jobs require comparable education, experience, and responsibility. City and county libraries in places where workers in other local government jobs receive higher pay for comparable work have been the focus of some of this attention. This issue is not addressed by the Equal Pay Act in a literal sense, although the purpose of the Act is to eliminate discrimination by providing for equal pay for equal work (Galloway 1978).

PERFORMANCE REVIEW

Some organizations tie performance appraisal ratings to pay increases, a practice watched by enforcement agencies to see whether employers consistently rate women and minorites lower than men and nonminorites. Affirmative action calls for employers to provide training and support to women and minorities to assist them in achieving successful performance (Mitnick 1977).

PENALITIES FOR NON-COMPLIANCE WITH EEO LAWS

The EEOC and the OFCCP are very serious about compliance with the law. Discrimination charges have been pressed against many employers and the employers have lost in most cases. Losing a discrimination case can be very costly in outright settlements, which may include back pay to entire groups of protected classes of workers in addition to the legal and administrative costs. Under the law, some specific actions which can result from conciliation with an employer can be 1) EEOC and OFCCP determination of personnel policies and affirmative action program content: 2) ratio hiring of women and minorities; and 3) back pay, hiring, promotion, and settlement payments. If conciliation is not achieved, there can be appropriate court actions, withholding of payments to contractors, or cancellation of contracts. Libraries can be affected by the withdrawal of federal funds in cases of discrimination, in addition to settlement and other costs.

BIBLIOGRAPHY

"Affirmative Action in Tucson: Library Develops Written Plan." *Library Journal* 103 (November 15, 1978): 2286.

Tucson has written an affirmative action plan, appointed an equal oppor tunity coordinator, and established a Library Affirmative Action Committee to identify any problem areas and recommend solutions.

American Library Association. Library Administration and Management Association. "EEOC Guidelines for Preventing Discriminatory Employment Practices." *American Libraries* 3 (December 1972): 1207-1209.

Describes the EEOC guidelines for recruiting and hiring by reviewing the equal employment opportunity legislation and the practices it prohibits. The applicability to libraries is summarized.

Brookmire, David A. "Designing and Implementing Your Company's Affirmative Action Plan." *Personnel Journal* 58 (April 1979): 232-237.

The plan should reflect the percent of females and minorities in the labor force in the area in which the organization is located. All levels of management must support the plan if it is to be successful, and training for supervisors in the meaning, philosophy and need for EEO is essential.

Cuesta, Yolanda. "Personnel and Employment: Affirmative Action." In *ALA Yearbook, 1980*, pp. 233-236. Chicago: American Library Association, 1980.

Under EEOC "Uniform Guidelines on Employee Selection Procedures," libraries will be required to validate the personnel selection procedures as long as disparate impact exists. The library literature related to affirmative action for the preceding year is reviewed, as well as legislation that affects libraries.

Cunningham, John. "Avoiding Common Pitfalls in Affirmative Action Programs." *Personnel Journal* 55 (March 1976): 125-127, 136.

It is to the advantage of most organizations to study their personnel practices to determine possible discrimination and needed corrective action even though they are not required under Title VII of the Civil Rights Act to establish any specific form of affirmative action. It makes good business sense to implement effective affirmative action programs before grievances arise and the federal government is called in to effect changes. Causes of failure of affirmative action programs are lack of commitment by the organization, inadequate allocation of resources for the EEO function, inadequate motivation of managers and superiors to implement EEO, and unsophisticated personnel programs. Suggestions for remedying these are given.

Dickinson, Elizabeth. "Affirmative Action Plans in Review: A Report from the Equal Employment Opportunity Subcommittee." *American Libraries* 10 (February 1979): 69-70.

Affirmative action plans can help protect library workers' employment rights and protect libraries against grievances and law suits because they are a way to put good personnel practices into orderly, written form. The American Library Association encourages the development of such plans and will review individual library plans for adequacy.

Dipboye, Robert L., Arvey, Richard D., and Terpstra, David E. "Equal Employment and the Interview." *Personnel Journal* 55 (October 1976): 520-522, 524.

Employers are relying more on the interview as a selection device since the courts have found other methods, such as intelligence tests, to be illegal under the Equal Opportunity laws. Interviewers' pitfalls are discussed: judging the qualifications of a candidate against an idealized stereotype; forgetting important information furnished during an interview; giving insufficient weight to favorable information; allowing initial impressions to influence decisions. Steps to improve the interview are discussed.

Galloway, Sue and Archuleta, Alyce. "Sex and Salary: Equal Pay for Comparable Work." *American Libraries* 9 (May 1978): 281-284.

Reference in Chapter 7 (Which see).

Gery, G. J. "Hiring Minorities and Women: The Selection Process." *Personnel Journal* 53 (December 1974): 906-909.

Organizations must seek out and hire minorities and women to meet the requirements of the law and must examine and change selection methods that are biased against these groups. The article discusses these problems and others concerned with test scores, interviews, and reference checks.

Hammer, Tove H. "Affirmative Action Programs: Have We Forgotten the First-Line Supervisor?" *Personnel Journal* 58 (June 1979): 384-389.

The first-line supervisors must implement affirmative action programs, but often are not involved in the interpretation of the corporate policy concerning them. As a result supervisors no longer have the last word in hiring decisions, may have their disciplinary actions reversed or overruled, and find productivity levels dropping as employees perceive affirmative action as differential treatment of the protected classes.

Higgins, James M. "A Manager's Guide to the Equal Employment Opportunity Laws." *Personnel Journal* 55 (August 1976): 406-411, 418.

An excellent outline of the EEO Laws that presents a summary of the content and requirements in a question and answer format. It covers discrimination, enforcement agencies, and penalties for noncompliance.

Miniter, John J. "Implications of Affirmative Action in Recruitment, Employment, and Termination of Personnel." *NC Libraries* 36 (Spring 1978): 16-20.

Affirmative action requires much more effort by organizations than does offering equal employment opportunities. The author suggests ideas for changes in library recruitment, performance appraisal, grievance procedures, and terminations.

Mitnick, Margery M. "Applications and References; Legal Considerations." *OLA Bulletin* 48 (October 1978): 29-38.

Sets forth the requirements of federal and Ohio state laws and do's and don't's associated with the use of application forms and reference checks as they relate to library practices. Useful guidelines are provided for employers responding to requests for reference checks.

Mitnick, Margery M. "Equal Employment Opportunity and Affirmative Action: A Managerial Training Guide." *Personnel Journal* 56 (October 1977): 492-497, 529.

Very good coverage of the EEO laws with explanations of types of discrimination and the employment practices most likely to be affected. Guidance is provided for those who must develop and write affirmative action programs.

Mood, Lester F. "Coping with Anti-Discrimination Laws." *Administrative Management* 41 (July 1980): 31-33,64,66.

Describes the most common violations of the laws, "evil motive", "differential treatment", and "disparate effect", and how organizations should deal with them. It is suggested that organizations keep detailed and accurate records on terminations of employees, selection of one job applicant over another, and other personnel actions. Employers charged with discrimination should analyze the charge, collect relevant data from their files, and cooperate with the investigating agency to resolve the problem.

Ohio Civil Rights Commission. *Questioning Applicants for Employment; A Guide for Application Forms and Interviews under the Ohio Fair Employment Practices Act.* Columbus, OH: The Commission, June 1970.

Provides a comprehensive list of lawful and unlawful inquiries that can be made before hiring, including age, race, sex, religion and place of work.

Omahan, Mary K. "The Legal Environment of the Interview." *OLA Bulletin* 48 (October 1978): 25-28.

Cites the interview as very vulnerable to discriminatory practices; employers must exercise care in the questions they ask and protect themselves against volunteered information that could serve as a basis for discrimination charges. Questions asked must be job related. An evaluation of the interview immediately after its completion is advised to avoid memory lapse. There should be a written record of the interview listing the questions asked and whether discriminatory information was volunteered and how it was handled.

Rudy, M. "Equity and Patterns of Library Governance." *Library Trends* 26 (Fall 1977): 181-193.

The bureaucratic and nontraditional forms of library governance such as participatory management are discussed in terms of their potential to achieve equity for women and minorities. The conclusion is that neither form of governance can ensure equity, but participation combined with the equal employment opportunity legislation has the potential to create an environment where equity can flourish.

Schiller, Anita. "The Disadvantaged Majority: Women Employed in Libraries." *American Libraries* 1 (April 1970): 345-349.

The median salary for women is lower than that for men by about $1500; men are about twice as likely as women to be chief librarians; and men who are not chief librarians tend to earn more than women who are. The top positions in the largest institutions are held by men.

The Supervisor's EEO Handbook; A Guide to Federal Antidiscrimination Laws and Regulations. Revised edition. New York: Executive Enterprises Publications Co., 1977.

Sets forth the essence of the laws and regulations and describes the compliance agencies involved for each.

10

LABOR RELATIONS

The movement to unionize, so prevalent in the public sector, has swept up librarians, causing rapid change in the relationships between workers and management even in libraries where the managers have been responsive to staff needs for better wages, working conditions and a part in decision making. Staff members feel they must join other workers in unions if they are to receive the same future benefits as other employees from their municipalities and other governing bodies. Professionals see union membership as strengthening their influence on the management of their work places, and they no longer view joining a union as unprofessional behavior.

BACKGROUND

The National Labor Relations Act of 1935 provided for employees in the private sector to organize and bargain collectively, but it was not until the 1960s and 70s that state enabling legislation extended protection for union activity in the public and nonprofit sectors. Because most librarians work in the public sector, there was little they could do in the way of collective bargaining until the late 1960s, but since that time their unionization has grown to the point that 20 percent of American librarians are represented by collective bargaining units (Kleingartner and Kennelly 1975).

There were movements toward unionization among librarians in earlier periods of adverse economic conditions, particularly in 1919 and in the late 1930s, when librarians saw that other workers were benefiting in the areas of wages, job security, and conditions of employment. The third movement came in the late 1960s, when the job situation had shifted from a seller's to a buyer's market and library budgets began to shrink. Salaries were lagging behind cost-of-living rises, and some libraries were reducing staff as they tried to maximize their resources (Michener 1974). At the same time it was being more widely recognized that workers need to have a voice in decisions that affect them.

Librarians have turned to trade unions or other bargaining units under two sets of conditions: 1) when the level of conflict between workers and management becomes intolerable or when workers feel frustrated by their inability to influence management decisions, and 2) when organization takes place in a class of employees of which librarians are a part, for example school librarians and teachers.

UNION AFFILIATIONS

The major library associations have remained aloof from the labor movement on the stated ground that it is unprofessional to engage in collective bargaining. In this they have been unlike similar professional organizations. The American Association of University Professors (AAUP) and the National Education Association (NEA) are examples of organizations that do bargain on behalf of their own employees.

With the American Library Association refusing to accept the bargaining role, librarians have lost an opportunity for a strong union of their own and find themselves scattered among the memberships of the AAUP, NEA, employee organizations, the American Federation of State, County, and Municipal Employees (AFSCME) and other established unions, depending upon whether they are academic, public, school, or special librarians.

PUBLIC LIBRARIES

An estimated 10 percent of public library employees are involved in collective bargaining, chiefly through the American Federation of State, County, and Municipal Employees (AFSCME). In some instances the membership is made up of library clerical and blue-collar workers and librarians; in others, just librarians; while in yet others, library employees are part of mixed bargaining units consisting of workers from different occupational categories of government. It has been found that librarians alone are too small a group to have much leverage as a bargaining unit. Library employees seek higher wages and salaries, improved working conditions, fair treatment, fringe benefits, job security, and a voice in decision making at the bargaining table, but are largely dependent upon others to achieve these benefits for them (Kleingartner and Kennelly, 1975).

The effects on public libraries have been in the areas of wages and salaries, personnel practices, and governance. Unions have negotiated for and received higher pay, including pay for employees' off-duty work, for time spent attending conferences, and for regular time used for union business. The library often winds up paying for much of the costs of unionization when union leaders are library employees. The costs to the library can also be very high for negotiations, grievance handling, and arbitration (Byam 1975).

The area of personnel practices has been heavily affected by unionization including promotions, transfers, hiring and firing, discipline, maintenance of personnel files, rules and procedures, staff development and training, and grievance and appeal procedures (SFPL 1978). In this area results have been good, in that library managements have had to put in writing such personnel policies and practices as selection and termination procedures. In hiring they have had to define qualifications carefully based on the requirements of the job (Guy 1980). If an MLS **is** required and the library is **not** prepared to accept a nonprofessional, the job qualifications must not state "MLS or equivalent experience" (Norwalk, 1979).

Unions limit a library manager's alternatives and options: rules and regulations cannot always be changed without union agreement; the library management must treat all staff equally in providing opportunities for training and development and conference attendance; seniority rather than qualifications may determine who gets a promotion; and job openings must be announced to all the staff.

Union grievance procedures can make a tremendous change in library management practices where managers are unaccustomed to dealing with contracts and union representatives or shop stewards. No longer does the manager or supervisor have all the power in the disputes and problems that arise between them and their employees. The management may be permitted to establish rules and regulations for the conduct of employees, but they may not be able to change regulations or add new ones without union review and approval. When grievances cannot be settled and must go to arbitration, the arbitrator, who is neither union nor management, can make decisions that affect library service yet be unaware of requirements for providing this service. An example would be a decision that only a custodian may lock the doors at night; if the custodian is unavailable for a later closing hour, the library would have to close early (Byam 1975).

In governance of libraries, unions provide a voice for employees, but also add one more layer of rules and regulations in addition to those of federal, state, and city governments, and boards of trustees. The amount of paper work or red tape also increases to include contracts, agreements, records of negotiation and arbitrations, and proposals and position papers of both sides (Mayer 1979).

The advantages to library employees include: 1) protection against arbitrary and capricious actions by local governments, boards, and administrators; 2) a sharing of the power to effect changes in the future direction of library development and service; 3) an assurance that sound personnel policies and practices are communicated in writing and will be implemented; and 4) higher salaries and improved fringe benefits.

SCHOOL LIBRARIES

With diminishing enrollments and tight economic conditions, public school teachers have increasingly joined unions to try to preserve their jobs and maintain their salary positions. School library media specialists have aligned themselves with teachers, naturally enough, since most of them nowadays came from the teacher ranks, have teacher certification and are an intrinsic part of the instructional program. Approximately one third of school media specialists are covered by collective bargaining with teachers or support staff such as nurses, playground directors, and counselors (Aaron 1978). Generally school personnel are seeking improved wages, hours, and other terms and conditions of employment, including job security.

The effects of unions on school library media centers are both advantageous and disadvantageous. The media specialist gains in salary and benefits as others (teachers) in the unit gain, and the center itself can gain if teachers understand the worth of library media programs and are willing to negotiate for improvements in the physical plant and the staff to operate it. In some instances, however, negotiators may bargain away some functions of library media programs as concessions for gaining something else they want. When teachers get union-negotiated free time during the day, the media specialist may become "baby-sitter" to their students. These disadvantages can result when the numbers of library media specialists are too small to exercise any power (Aaron 1978).

Union membership of library media specialists can mean that they do not take work home, work after school without pay, nor attend meetings outside of school hours. It can also result in tuition paid for course work, and released time for workshops and conferences. There is no doubt that unionization is spreading among school librarians who see no other way to gain the benefits they seek.

SPECIAL LIBRARIES

Fewer than one percent of special librarians are unionized. In cases where they are, it is as employees of unionized companies or as employees of federal libraries. There are very few data available on collective bargaining among special librarians (Kleingartner and Kennelly 1975).

BIBLIOGRAPHY

Aaron, Shirley L. "The Media Supervisor and Collective Bargaining." *Drexel Library Quarterly* 14 (July 1978): 95-101.

The media supervisor must decide whether affiliation with a union will enable her to strengthen the supervisory program to serve better the needs of the district based upon several factors including whether 1) there is a community of interests with the union, 2) the union is concerned about the central issues of providing media services 3) the union provides a broader power base to the supervisor, and 4) the supervisor will have a voice in the policies of the union. If a union has been accepted, the supervisor can work to assure that teachers realize the value of media services and will help to negotiate items concerned with media into the contract.

Brandwein, Larry. "From Confrontation To Coexistence." *Library Journal* 104 (March 15, 1979): 681-683.

A recounting of events of confrontation between union and management of the Brooklyn Public Library and subsequent settlement of differences, and a decade of working together to assure fairness. The key to the change was mutual trust and respect, with each side keeping its word and jointly working out problems.

Byam, Milton S. "Implications for Public Libraries." In *Collective Bargaining in Libraries*, Frederick A. Schlipf, editor, pp. 117-121. Urbana-Champaign, IL: University of Illinois, Allerton Park Institute, 1975.

In public libraries, when unions become part of the governance they may not share in management's mission to meet the needs of the public for service; likewise, arbitrators may not understand how the libraries must operate to provide services and will make decisions that curtail them. Cost of unionization is very high to libraries and must be paid by them. On the positive side unionization has resulted in more evenhanded treatment of staff by management and municipalities, and union leaders generally have been responsive to the library's needs.

Cooper, B.S. "Collective Bargaining Comes to School Middle Management." *Phi Delta Kappan*, 58 (October 1976): 203.

The American Federation of School Administrators (AFSA) of the AFL-CIO was founded in 1976 to represent principals, supervisors, and other middle managers. Unionization of supervisors/administrators in education is unique in the American labor movement; industrial supervisors are forbidden to bargain by the Taft-Hartley Act of 1947 and federally employed supervisors are likewise limited by Executive Order 10988 of 1962.

Frantz, John C. "The Trustees and Labor-Management Relations." In *The Library Trustee; A Practical Guidebook*, Virginia G. Young, editor, pp. 38-41. New York: R. R. Bowker Co., 1978.

Advises the trustees to become familiar with the laws authorizing employee organizations and the scope of collective bargaining in their states and describes the negotiating process which results in a final agreement or contract between the board and the union.

Goldstein, Melvin S. *Collective Bargaining in the Field of Librarianship*. Brooklyn, N.Y.: Pratt Institute, 1968.

A history of library unionization in the U.S. and a summary of the current status as determined from a survey of large public, academic, and governmental libraries. The terms of contracts current in 1968 are provided.

Guy, Jeniece. "Mediation, Arbitration, and Inquiry." In *ALA Yearbook*, pp. 205-206. Chicago: American Library Association, 1980.

The status of librarians in unions should be defined when they are part of a larger collective bargaining unit; library personnel procedures should be in writing, particularly those dealing with hiring, termination, and defining qualifications for particular jobs.

Jaffe, Martin E. "Solidarity Forever: How To Negotiate Your First Labor Contract and Live Happily Ever After or Until the Contract Expires (Whichever Comes First)." *Library Journal* 104 (October 15, 1979): 2172-2173.

Do's and don'ts of negotiation: do get management to initial your recognition clause granting formal recognition of your group to bargain; do read your initial proposals to the management negotiation team; never mail your proposals to the management team before the first session; do let your chief negotiator present your agreements and respond to management's counter-proposals; do bargain for certain "must" benefits such as salary, a fair grievance procedure, and job security.

Kleingartner, Archie and Kennelly, Jean R. "Employee Relations in Libraries: The Current Scene." In *Collective Bargaining in Libraries*, Frederick A. Schlipf, Editor, pp. 1-22. Urbana-Champaign, IL, University of Illinois, Allerton Park Institute, 1975.

Brief history of the involvement of librarians in collective bargaining; a discussion of professions and their reasons for joining unions; and the types of organizations that represent library employees. The goals of library professionals are of two types: 1) those related to pay, working conditions, treatment, fringe benefits, and job security, and 2) the longer-range ones related to professional growth, career satisfaction, the ability to deal with clients and be recognized as professionals, and to have a voice in critical management decisions.

Mayer, Albert I. "Unions: Plus or Minus?" *Wilson Library Bulletin*, 54 (December 1979): 242-243.

The author's view is that librarians are better off not to unionize because (1) there is only so much money available to run the library and the costs to the library for negotiators' fees and other expenses take money that could go to librarians' salaries; (2) the red tape generated by contracts, negotiations, and other regulations must be dealt with; (3) the library can no longer send people to conferences and share expenses with them because it shows partiality in treatment; and (4) negotiators sometimes bargain away benefits the board would have been willing to provide or settle for less than the board would have given.

Michener, Roger E. "Unions and Libraries: The Spheres of Intellect and Politics." *Southeastern Librarian* (Winter 1974): 15-25.

Libraries are intellectual institutions contributing to the discovery and teaching of truth—in this role they are not political. They are political in that most are supported by the state and assist in the training of people for various roles in society. Unions are political in their efforts to gain power and influence in an adversary position. Libraries, unlike manufacturing organizations, have limited resources, and unions can help them gain only limited economic benefits while distracting them from their primary intellectual pursuits.

"Norwalk Nonpro Gets Job Created for M.L.S. Grad." *Library Journal*, 104, (March 15, 1979): 670; "Norwalk Union Backs Pro Bumped by Nonprofessional." *Library Journal* 104 (July 1979): 1410-1411.

A union files a complaint against the Norwalk Public Library charging it with violation of the union contract in designing a job to fit a new M.L.S graduate working at the library under the Comprehensive Employment and Training Act (CETA). A nonprofessional with seniority also applied for the job, which had been posted as open to an M.L.S. holder or one of equivalent experience, but was not selected. The State Board of Mediation and Arbitration agreed with the union and ordered the appointment of the nonprofessional. The union subsequently took up the defense of the CETA employee and filed a grievance on her behalf.

"SFPL Union Claims Big Management Concessions." *Library Journal*, 103 (April 1, 1978): 704-705.

The Librarians' Guild of the Civil Service Association, which represents the staff of the San Francisco Public Library, signed a Memorandum of Understanding (MOU) with the administration which provided for shop stewards to try to resolve grievances at the lowest possible level, to pay staff for off-duty work, to give the staff a voice in policy making and to improve orientation programs. The union agreed not to strike or authorize a work stoppage while the MOU is in effect and acknowledged the library's right to revise performance standards.

Weatherford, John. "Collective Bargaining and the Academic Librarian, 1976-1979." *Library Journal*, 105 (February 15, 1980): 481-482.

Librarians in large multicampus systems who have bargaining agents are aligned with many other employees including faculty, coaches, counselors, and various administrators and are not exclusively identified with faculty. Librarians show little inclination to form bargaining units of their own unless faculty bargaining does not exist and appears remote. In some academic institutions faculty are bargaining without librarians and the librarians are forming their own units. Where librarians are aligned with faculty, they often do not get equal benefits such as traditional tenure, faculty rank, and equal salaries.

Weatherford, John W. "Hidden Costs of Collective Bargaining." *American Libraries*, 9 (May 1978): 273.

Prolonged bargaining is expensive and diverts funds from the benefit of the whole to a few cases. Bargaining, grievance procedures, and arbitration are costs the employer must pass on to the employees. Union dues are a direct cost to employees. A union of only librarians is small and weak; librarians as part of a larger unit must compete as a minority.

11

SCHOOL LIBRARY MEDIA CENTERS

The 80,000 school libraries and/or media centers in public and private schools make up the largest class of small library in the United States (Little 1980), and they differ markedly from other small libraries in clientele, purpose, and information delivery. Their directors, moreover, have responsibilities—to assist learners on a one-to-one basis or in small groups, to participate in curriculum development, and to produce as well as to identify and purchase instructional materials—that are markedly different from those of other special librarians. Also, to a greater extent than the public librarian, the school library media specialist must work directly and individually with people on many levels: students, teachers, and administrators (both school and district). He or she assists staff which may be composed primarily of students or community volunteers, for the school library media specialist quite often works as the sole professional in the library media center. In no other type of library does the librarian need more sensitivity and skill in the management of personal relationships.

THE ROLE OF THE LIBRARY MEDIA SPECIALIST

The role of the library media specialist is many faceted and professionally demanding. It is also still evolving, along with the evolution of the school library media center itself, from a study room containing a limited (and often random) collection of printed supplemental materials into a central laboratory of learning resources and specialized equipment whose use is integrated into the instructional program.

The specialist quit the "support staff" category to become a member of the instructional team by actively providing learner-centered instruction and guidance, assisting teachers by acquiring material tailored for specific classes, serving on the curriculum committees, and building and organizing a multi-media collection in a center that supports both students' and teachers' needs (Bock 1977). One might argue that school librarians have done these things for years. This was true for the schools that had librarians and to the extent of the resources; but until money became available, first under the National Defense Education Act and then under the Elementary and Secondary Education Act of 1965, many schools had no libraries, and many others had such very poor ones that they were able to provide only limited supplemental enrichment to classroom teachers who were pretty well locked into rigid textbook teaching.

The impetus provided by the ALA's promulgation of Standards for School Library Programs (1960) and the subsequent five year long demonstration of exemplary library media center programs by the Knapp School Libraries Project (Fite 1980), may well have been responsible for the increase in federal and state funds that enabled public school libraries to come into their own in the schools' instructional programs. By 1978, 95 percent of U.S. public school children were enrolled in schools that had library media centers; and these centers employed a total of 82,000 staff—an average of 1.15 for each school—who were certified as librarians, audiovisual specialists, media specialists, or classroom teachers. These figures reflect the tremendous growth that has taken place in little more than a dozen years.

The library media specialist has wide scope and many responsibilities. He or she must design and implement a program of services; consult with teachers and staff on mission, goals, and priorities for the center; guide and direct students in their use of materials and equipment; evaluate services and redesign programs as needed; administer the center; direct and develop staff; consult with the principal and district supervisor; and work cooperatively with other libraries to share resources. The library media specialist is at once a designer, manager, consultant, teacher, provider of services, and human relations practitioner (Martin and Carson 1978). Success in the job requires 1) managing time through scheduling, 2) planning to meet the objectives of the school's program for integration and utilization of learning resources, 3) acquiring and organizing materials, 4) communicating with students, staff, and teachers, and 5) managing an active and busy learning center. The school library media specialist today functions in a central role in the continuing education of teachers in the production of materials and utilization of media from books and films to simulations and computers.

RELATIONSHIP WITH STUDENTS

Library media specialist's first responsibility is to the students, who need the resources of the center and the expert knowledge of the media specialist in their quest for information and learning. The specialist guides individual and group independent learning projects and works in partnership with the classroom teacher to teach search and study skills which will be used lifelong by students. The central question is how best to facilitate learning. It is accomplished by providing a wide variety of materials in various formats, giving students opportunities for experimentation, being a personal resource and learning facilitator, and providing an environment that promotes learning. These are essential; but the library media specialist also cultivates a service philosophy that is student centered and is willing to share himself or herself as a person who has feelings, opinions, likes, and dislikes. Such a person can let it be known when behavior is unacceptable in the center while simultaneously indicating acceptance of the person and care for his feelings and opinions (Rogers, 1969). The library media specialist must understand how the process of learning appears to the student.

The ultimate goal of the library media specialist is to foster independent learners who take increasing responsibility for their own education. More than any other teacher, the library media specialist takes special responsibility for the gifted and talented student who must be challenged beyond the bounds of the curriculum. In fact, in a number of school districts, library media specialists have formal responsibility for the entire gifted program. They have made outstanding contributions to the education of handicapped and retarded children as well.

Through teaching, encouragement, and support, the specialist helps many students to acquire the knowledge and research skills they will need for continuing learning during the rest of their lives for jobs, civic and political involvement, hobbies, and recreation (Dane 1979).

RELATIONSHIP WITH TEACHERS

The librarian and the teachers are colleagues and collaborators in the learning process. They realize that students learn in many different ways—by reading, listening, viewing, and doing—and that a variety of materials are needed to facilitate the process. As team members, teachers and center directors work together (Dane 1979) and are in continuous communication about assignments and projects if the educational program is to function smoothly (Martin and Carson 1978).

For their part, teachers have a responsibility to require students to use the library media center for preparation of assignments and for individual projects, and to encourage students to experiment with different media and to try new approaches to learning. On the other hand, the library media specialist must approach teachers on curriculum development and planning, then work with them to select and produce the materials they will need. Serving as a curriculum consultant is time consuming and can be difficult for the library media specialist who may not have subject knowledge in particular instructional areas; but it pays dividends as instructional programs and media services mesh to improve the quality of education (Grazier 1979). Library media specialists have an opportunity to evaluate students, especially their reading, listening, and group leadership skills, and can share their insights with teachers and help prescribe for individual students.

If the media specialist is appointed to the curriculum committee by the principal, as happens in many schools, he or she can provide valuable assistance as courses are designed by advising the committee on the availability of materials already in the center, what other materials are commercially available at what cost, how much time is required to produce materials locally, and whether the facilities of the center can accommodate proposed activities. At the same time teachers can assist the specialist in selecting materials and equipment. Better selections and greater utilization of materials by teachers and students results (Bock 1977).

RELATIONSHIP WITH THE PRINCIPAL

If the media center is to function effectively, the school principal must understand its value to the curriculum and to learning and be totally committed to its support. Many principals, unfortunately, have little real knowledge of, or experience with, library media centers. The library media specialist has a responsibility to keep the principal informed about the work of the center, and the improvements necessary for conformance with state and national standards, staffing requirements, and expenditures (Martin and Carson 1978). A weekly or monthly written report on use of the center, including accomplishments, problems, and faculty needs for materials, will help the principal understand the function of a media center and what is required to maintain its viability (Rosenberg 1978).

The principal and the library media specialist must, through discussion, develop clear agreement in three important areas, the first being the policies, goals, and objectives of the center. These must be in harmony with those for the school as a whole.

The second has to do with the definition of the specialist's role. To what extent will he or she participate in curriculum development? Attend teacher and parent-teacher meetings? Confer with parents? May the specialist and a teacher approach one another directly to initiate a project, or must they go through a department head? Who decides what the chief emphasis of the specialist's job should be, and what the reasonable workload? Who judges the specialist's performance to determine ratings and promotions?

Third, it is important that the principal and the library media specialist work together, or at least keep one another closely informed, in establishing relationships with the local public and other libraries and with community groups. As declining school age populations threaten acquisitions budgets based on per capita enrollments, school library media specialists are seeking new users who range from preschool children to senior citizens. (This trend can be coupled beautifully with the increasing emphasis on lifetime learning.) They are also realizing that it is necessary to join cooperative information and resource sharing networks (Baker 1980). As all local officials examine budgets, they become eager to eliminate duplicative services. In California, for example, demonstrations of cooperation between school and public libraries have been funded with the object of eliminating duplication while maintaining and improving services (California 1980).

It is vital that the center have a written selection policy, approved and supported by the principal. It provides the backbone of the defense of selections that community groups or individuals may attempt to censor, and it serves as a useful guide in acquiring materials. It should ensure that both sides of an issue will be covered, indicate the scope of selection to support the curriculum and programs, and define the quality of materials to be acquired to assure accuracy and excellence.

RELATIONSHIP WITH THE DISTRICT DIRECTOR

District library media directors (the preferred term over supervisor or consultant) are in a position to provide leadership, influence the quality of the instructional program, and assist the school specialist to upgrade his center by virtue of their access to superintendents and boards of education as part of the district administration. They can be the catalysts who bring together teachers, administrators, library media specialists, and the people of the community to develop quality media programs in every school (Strack 1979).

The director should be concerned with personnel practices in the district, assist principals to employ qualified librarians or media specialists, promote staff development and continuing education in each school, and advise principals on the wise use of professional capabilities.

Directors can assist each school library media center to meet district goals. They can help to implement programs and solve problems. They can speak for all schools at district headquarters and in meetings where budgetary and other management decisions are made (Bingham 1979).

The district director has responsibility for the quality of the total instructional media program for the district, whereas the principal at the building level must assure smooth operation of all programs within the building, including that of the library media center. To minimize potential conflict, the media library specialist should consult the principal on all problems or questions concerning the interface of the media staff with teachers, students, and the community; and on matters of budget, the instructional program, and the use of the center.

In today's schools library media specialists are well educated, many having teacher certification as well as library media credentials. They enjoy considerable autonomy, obviating the need for constant, close supervision by district administrators. The latter are, however, valuable as advisors and sources of information about new materials, equipment, and techniques. They know what resources can be borrowed by one school from another and will play a leading role in integrating the school centers into area library networks and cooperatives. A major role is initiator and organizer of staff development opportunities for mixed groups of teachers, administrators, library media, reading and other specialists.

ADMINISTRATION AND STAFFING

The school library media specialist must be administrator as well as teacher and manager. He or she must deal with the ever-pressing tasks of identification, selection, and processing materials; repair of equipment; record keeping; and report writing.

Assessment of new materials and equipment involves time and sometimes travel to a district center, and, although most school districts have central facilities for preparing and cataloging materials, the school specialist must still receive them and maintain the catalogs and other keys to the collections necessary for effective patron use. Circulation records must be kept, and records of material out for repair or on loan outside the school. There are records to be maintained to meet state department accreditation. The burden of record keeping alone requires clerical support staff in most centers (Martin and Carson 1978).

Although more than 80 percent of public schools now have the services of a library media specialist, many are less than fulltime in one school. Many elementary schools share a specialist and are dependent upon part-time clerical staff or volunteers to keep the center open and maintain at least a basic program. Where there are support staff, the professional must plan the work so that tasks and worker qualifications match, reserving to himself the tasks of evaluation and selection of material, working with teachers, and guiding students. Well supervised aides and volunteers can do a fine job and the work will get done by those who can do it best, but the staff will be motivated by a library media specialist who values their work.

VOLUNTEER ASSISTANCE

In some schools it may be the case that only through volunteer help can the library media center even remain open, while in others volunteers can make it possible to expand services or offer new programs. The library media specialist can recruit volunteers by direct contact, or through the school administration and the parent-teacher organization, or by advertising in school and community newspapers. Many school districts have a volunteer office that solicits and helps to train people.

Before making any contacts, however, the library media specialist should draw up a plan for utilization of volunteers. The plan should include organizing the work of the center so that volunteers can work on a part-time basis; preparing a job-training program; and writing guidelines to inform volunteers of school policies and center procedures.

The training program is the key to the success of a volunteer program. Schools cannot always select from the individuals who volunteer, but must simply accept those who come. In most cases, although they may be very dedicated and eager to help, volunteers don't have all the necessary skills. The training program must be designed so that volunteers understand their responsibilities; and they must feel needed, welcome, and useful (Stanton 1978). The volunteers will regard the library media specialist as the expert and as the person who plans what they are to do.

Community volunteers who can make a commitment of time on specific days of the week can share routine jobs that must be done regularly; for example, two or more can share responsibility for maintaining files, cleaning equipment, or shelving books. But it is important to remember that satisfaction and a sense of real contribution is the only coin in which these workers are paid, so they must do more than drudgery if they are to stay. One-to-one work with children is one of the most satisfying tasks for many volunteers. While making valuable contributions to the library media program, these adult volunteers gain a better understanding of the school—

and, if they are also parents, an appreciation of the quality of the education provided their sons and daughters. They can then speak to school needs in the community and serve in a valuable public relations role (Crisler 1979). Ideally, the library media specialist can treat them as regular staff members would be treated, evaluating their work and seeing to it that they carry out the assignments.

STUDENT ASSISTANCE

Students during their free periods and before and after school can also assist in the center; many schools give credit for this and consider it a learning experience. As with adult volunteers, the director must plan their work and provide training. While the center benefits from their work, the students gain useful knowledge about libraries: how resources are made available, how services are provided, and how to handle and care for materials and equipment.

Students can be treated differently from parents and other adult volunteers in that they can be screened according to grade level, how well they maintain their school work, and their performance in the center. Fairly strict guidelines for selection can be maintained. In some situations students are paid for their efforts. If they are working as part of their vocational education program, the students are treated as staff members and are expected to work regular schedules and have their performance evaluated.

Students will take pride in their work and gain in maturity from assuming responsibilities and achieving results. A student aide job is an honor which brings respect and responsibility. Student work must be monitored to assure that it is done completely and well, but mistakes should be treated as learning experiences. Certificates recognizing good performance will reward student volunteers for their contributions.

Other chapters of this book should be consulted for fuller treatment of topics related to staff management, in particular those on communicating with staff, supervision of people, staff development, and performance appraisal.

BIBLIOGRAPHY

Baker, D. Philip. "School Libraries and Media Programs." In *ALA Yearbook*,pp. 276-280. Chicago: American Library Association, 1980.

> School librarians are seeking new ways to deliver services to students and teachers and to enlarge their clientele to include preschoolers through senior citizens. The American Association of School Librarians and the Association for Educational Communication and Technology are cooperating at the national and state levels to develop improved services through common goals.

Bingham, Rebecca T. "Components of Effective Supervision at the District Level." *School Media Quarterly* 7 (Spring 1979): 191-194.

> Supervisors are in a position to provide leadership at the district level to achieve planned change and to establish new ways of providing services as enrollments continue to decline and budgets become tighter. A humanistic approach to supervision is advocated in which library media specialists have challenging and satisfying work as a result of job enrichment and other motivational action by the supervisor, who also helps them deal with problems and meet the challenges of their demanding roles.

Bock, D. Joleen. "Role of the Library Media Specialist in Curriculum Development." *Ohio Media Spectrum* 29 (October 1977): 57-59.

> The library media specialist should be a member of the curriculum committee, if possible, to advise on what materials are available to support instructional programs. The media center collection will benefit from the subject knowledge of the teachers, and teachers who participate in selection of materials will make greater use of the center.

"California Puts LSCA into School Library Coop." *Library Journal* 105 (September 1, 1980): 1694.

Seven projects have been funded with LSCA money to demonstrate how public and school libraries can work together to provide service at less cost.

Crisler, E. "Media Center; A View from the Principal's Office." *Mississippi Libraries*, 43 (Autumn 1979): 133-136.

The media center must provide more diverse services than the traditional school library, including the teaching of basic skills. Every student should have access to many types of media and learn to use the center for information and entertainment. The center director can assist teachers in responding to state-mandated changes in curriculum and, through use of volunteers, communicate the school's needs to the community.

Dane, Chase. "Managing the School Media Library." In *Current Concepts in Library Management*, Martha Boaz, editor, pp. 96-130. Littleton, CO: Libraries Unlimited, Inc., 1979.

Describes the functions of the school library, the roles of the building library media specialist, the district supervisor, volunteers, and student assistants. The media center concept is discussed with emphasis on helping students learn through many types of media.

Darling, Richard L. "District Level Support of School Media Center Programs." In *Excellence in School Media Programs*, Thomas J. Galvin, Margaret M. Kimmel, and Brenda H. White, editors, pp. 95-100. Chicago: American Library Association, 1980.

District media directors are on the staff of the superintendent and can influence policy and decision making on behalf of the media program. They can help new schools establish media centers, orient new staff, and assist with selection and purchase of materials. At the district level they can sponsor new media workshops, train library aides, and provide training to teachers on the use of new media.

Downes, Valerie J. "Who's Who in Problem Solving." *Illinois Libraries* 60 (September 1978): 594-596.

To whom does the library media specialist turn when problems arise and he/she is accountable to both the principal and the district supervisor? This author recommends that the principal be consulted on problems dealing with teachers, students, parents, curriculum, budget, and activities in the building. The district supervisor is knowledgeable about the district's overall media program and can be consulted on decisions that affect it.

Fite, Alice E. *"The Essential Elementary School Library Media Center." In Excellence in School Media Programs*, Thomas J. Galvin, Margaret M. Kimmel, and Brenda H. White, editors, pp. 85-94. Chicago: American Library Association, 1980.

Reviews the change in school libraries to multimedia centers, noting the influence of standards and the Knapp School Libraries Project on the development of an awareness of the need for school library media centers. Covered are current constraints of budget, decreased enrollments, and taxpayer resistance to increased taxes.

Grazier, Margaret H. "The Curriculum Consultant Role of the School Library Media Specialist." *Library Trends* 28 (Fall 1979): 263-279.

A review of research studies and their findings. Traces the evolution of school librarianship from a supportive role to teachers to that of curriculum developers and integrators of all kinds of media. Discusses the competencies of the library media specialist and perceptions of the role by teachers, administrators and media professionals.

Little, Robert D. "Public School Library Media Centers." In *The Bowker Annual of Library and Book Trade Information*, pp. 395-400. New York: R.R. Bowker Co., 1980.

In 1978-79 there were more than 81,000 public schools with library media centers serving over 40 million students. This is a decrease from 1974 levels, when nearly 44 million were served by 85,000 centers. Expenditures increased for books, periodicals, and salaries; although fewer books were purchased and expenditures decreased for audio-visual materials. There were 1.15 certified staff members for every media center in the fall of 1978, for a total of nearly 82,000.

Mancall, Jacqueline C. and Barber, Raymond W. "Management by Objectives as a Process to Facilitate Supervision and Staff Development." *Drexel Library Quarterly* 14 (July 1978): 3-11.

The application of management by objectives (MBO) to a school district, which, having no profit motive, is measured by its effectiveness. The media supervisor should evaluate services constantly and assure that every staff member has clearly stated objectives that contribute to and support other units of the school program. A brief description is given of the use of MBO.

Martin, Betty and Carson, Ben. *The Principal's Handbook on the School Library Media Center.* Hamden, CT: Library Professional Publications, 1978. "What is the Role of the Teacher?": 52-60.

The teacher is a team member in the learning process, which utilizes media of all kinds. With the assistance of the library media specialist, teachers plan their instructional programs, encourage students to use multimedia, and develop the media collection in their subject areas.

"What is the Role of the Library Media Specialist?": 61-69.

The library media specialist assists the faculty in planning for the use of media in the curriculum, provides services to students to encourage them to learn to find and use information and experiment with different media, and works with the principal to build an excellent media program. The library media specialist is designer, teacher, consultant, evaluator, administrator, and communicator.

"How Should the Principal Relate to the Staff of the Media Center?": 77-89.

The principal and the library media specialist should work together to build the school library media center program. The library media specialist should keep the principal informed of the goals of the center, improvements needed, and performance. The two should meet frequently, agree on policies, and review rules and regulations.

"How Should the Media Center be Administered?": 106-120.

The library media specialist must select materials and equipment based on a written policy, make work assignments to the staff, maintain records on acquisitions and circulation, and prepare regular reports on center use and activities, problems, plans with teachers, needs, and purchases.

Rogers, Carl. *Freedom to Learn.* Columbus, OH: Charles E. Merrill Publishing Co., 1969.

A discussion of student-centered teaching, in which students are valued as persons, trusted to learn on their own, and accepted as they are by the teachers. The teachers are described as facilitators of learning who let their own feelings and opinions be known, thus becoming real persons to their students. The results of this kind of teaching are students who are more responsible and creative, and teachers who experience challenge and meaningful relationships.

Rosenberg, Marc J. "Strategies for Improving the Library Media Specialist — Principal Relationship." *Illinois Libraries* 60 (March 1978): 291-293.

To gain the support of the principal, the media specialist should assist the faculty in curriculum development and support their classroom activities with materials; know and support school policies; understand the financial situation and budgets; educate and inform the principal on new materials and solicit his/her suggestions; communicate with the PTA, the school board, and community groups about the school library media program; and display a positive attitude about his/her job and abilities.

Smith, Nathan M. "The Librarian as Counselor: Detroit Revisited." *Top of the News* 34 (Summer 1978): 323-329.

A review of a workshop on librarians as counselors, especially to young adults. Emphasis of counseling is to help healthy individuals function at higher levels through listening and understanding. Some pointers on counseling are given, including when referrals should be made to a medical or other professional.

Stanton, Vida C. "Volunteers: Another View; How Do the Volunteers Feel About Their Work?" *Wisconsin Library Bulletin* 74 (September 1978): 235-236.

Volunteers feel they are wanted, needed, and useful. They gain insight into the expectations and goals of their school and are able to speak positively in discussions about it.

Strack, Robert C. "The District Media Supervisor: Personnel, Planning, and Technical Duties are Major." *Wisconsin Library Bulletin* 75 (May 1979): 115-116.

A primary function of the district supervisor is to serve as consultant to the school principal for personnel management of the media center: selection, hiring, evaluation, and staff development. Another role is serving as catalyst in developing a library media program that meets the needs of the district, by bringing together teachers, administrators, library media specialist, students, and parents. A third responsibility, providing technical services to the individual centers, can be very time consuming and tends to shut out the other two, unless priorities are set and time allotted to long-range values rather than details.

APPENDIX 1

OUR TOWN PUBLIC LIBRARY
Performance Appraisal
Professional Librarian

NAME: _____

Period of Review: From _____

To _____

Reviewed by: _____

Job Title: _____ Prepared by: _____

This appraisal was read by me and discussed with my supervisor:

_____
Signed*

JOB RESPONSIBILITIES	Performance Rating
Plan and organize work of the group	1 2 3 4
Communicate with staff and peers concerning ongoing work and to the public	1 2 3 4
Perform administrative duties (budgets, schedules and paper work)	1 2 3 4
Supervise the work of others	1 2 3 4
Demonstrate leadership traits and behaviors (flexibility, tolerance, integrity, ability to guide and motivate others)	1 2 3 4

*Staff member's signature does not imply agreement

Example 1. Appraisal Form: Professional

PERFORMANCE REVIEW FOR THE PAST YEAR   Progress
A. Major Performance Goals
   1)
   2)
   3)
   4)

B. Development Activities (Courses, Training, Workshops, Reading, etc.)
   1)
   2)
   3)

OVERALL PERFORMANCE RATING (Circle one) 1 2 3 4

Explanation of ratings:

1 — Excels in all aspects. Takes the initiative, is innovative, and exceeds goals.

2 — Excels in most aspects. Occasionally exceeds goals.

3 — Good overall performance. Occasionally misses deadlines and sometimes falls short of goals.

4 — Poor performance. Seldom achieves goals and usually falls short on performance.

SUPERVISOR'S COMMENTS
_____
_____

FUTURE DEVELOPMENT PLANS
_____
_____

STAFF MEMBER'S COMMENTS
_____
_____

PERFORMANCE GOALS FOR COMING YEAR
   A. _____
   B. _____

AN EQUAL EMPLOYMENT OPPORTUNITY EMPLOYER

Example 1. (Continued)

```
┌─────────────────────────────────────────────────┐
│              OUR TOWN PUBLIC LIBRARY            │
│                Performance Appraisal            │
│                Non-Professional Staff           │
│                                                 │
│   NAME: _____ Period of Review: From __ To __
│                                                 │
│   Job No. and Title _____ Prepared by: _____
│                                                 │
│   Reviewed by: _____ This appraisal was ready by
│   me and discussed with my supervisor:          │
│                                                 │
│   _____   │
│                    Signed**                     │
│                                                 │
│   STAFF MEMBER'S COMMENTS: _____    │
│   _____   │
│   _____   │
│   _____   │
│   _____   │
│                                                 │
│   FUTURE PERFORMANCE GOALS: _____     │
│                                                 │
│       1. _____       │
│                                                 │
│       2. _____       │
│                                                 │
│       3. _____       │
│                                                 │
│   FUTURE DEVELOPMENT PLANS: _____     │
│   _____   │
│   _____   │
│                                                 │
│   _____                                 │
│   **Staff member's signature does not imply agreement.
└─────────────────────────────────────────────────┘
```

Example 2. Appraisal Form: Nonprofessional

ELEMENTS OF EVALUATION	Performance Rating*
	(Circle one)
Degree to which work is accurate and thorough and meets standards of quality	1 2 3 4
Degree to which person is knowledgeable about the work based on experience, education, and training	1 2 3 4
Adaptability of person: accepts changes and willingness to try new methods	1 2 3 4
Degree to which responsibility for work is assumed without need for close supervision	1 2 3 4
Degree to which person works cooperatively and harmoniously with others	1 2 3 4
Ability of person to perform expected quantities of work in a reasonable time period	1 2 3 4

DEVELOPMENT ACTIVITIES COMPLETED

_____

_____

_____

SUPERVISOR'S OVERALL RATING: (Circle one) 1 2 3 4

Comments: _____

_____

_____

*1 — Outstanding 3 — Satisfactory
 2 — Excellent   4 — Unsatisfactory

Example 2. (Continued)

APPENDIX 2

DATE: _____

OUR TOWN PUBLIC LIBRARY
EMPLOYMENT APPLICATION

NAME: _____ Telephone: _____ Social Security # _____

ADDRESS: _____

PERSONAL DATA

Have you been convicted of a felony or misdemeanor or forfeited bond within the past seven years? If so, explain. _____ Yes _____ No

_____

Position Desired: _____ Salary expected: $ _____

Work Schedule Desired: _____ Parttime _____

Are there reasons why you cannot work during evening or weekend hours? _____ Yes _____ No

Do you have a physical handicap that should be given consideration in job placement? _____ Yes _____ No

If yes, describe _____

EDUCATION (List all educational institutions attended; last one first)

	Name and Address	Degree	Dates Attended	Date Graduated
High school or vocational school				

Colleges	_____ _____ _____ _____
	_____ _____ _____ _____
	_____ _____ _____ _____

Library School	_____ _____ _____ _____
	_____ _____ _____ _____
	_____ _____ _____ _____

MILITARY SERVICE RECORD   Principal   Branch of
                                       Assignments   Skills   Rank   Service

From _____

To _____

Dates of employment _____ Final Salary $ _____

                    Month/Year to Month/Year

Job Responsibilities _____

_____

Reason for leaving _____

May we contact your employer? _____ Yes _____ No

RECOGNITION

Describe awards, special training, volunteer work or other accomplishments associated with your work that could be important to your employment consideration:

_____

_____

REFERENCES

List names, addresses, and telephone numbers of three employment or school references that the OUR TOWN PUBLIC LIBRARY has permission to contact:

Name   Street   City   State   Zip Code   Telephone   Years Known

_____

_____

_____

EMPLOYMENT (List most recent employer first; use extrs sheets if necessary)

Library or organization _____

Address _____

Dates of employment _____ Final Salary $ _____

Month/Year to Month/Year

Job Responsibilities _____

_____

Reason for Leaving _____

May we contact your present employer? _____ Yes _____ No

Library or organization _____

Address _____

Dates of employment _____ Final Salary $ _____

                Month/Year to Month/Year

Job Responsibilities _____

_____

Reason for leaving _____

May we contact your employer? _____ Yes _____ No

Library or organization _____

Address _____

_____

Signed _____

              AN EQUAL EMPLOYMENT
            OPPORTUNITY EMPLOYER

INDEX

Aaron, Shirley L., 98–99
Absenteeism, 35, 53, 86
Academic Library, 23, 66, 101, 103
Adult Learners, 4
Advertising, 84, 112
Affirmative Action, 6, 77–84, 87, 89–93
Age Discrimination in Employment Act
(*See* Antidiscrimination Laws)
Alcoholism, 30
American Association of School Librarians, 114
American Association of University Professors, 96
American Federation of School Administrators
(*See* Labor Unions)
American Federation of State, County, and Municipal Employees
(*See* Labor Unions)
American Library Association, 52, 83, 86, 91, 96, 106
  Equal Employment Opportunity Subcommittee, 83, 90
  Library Administration & Management Association, 89
  Office of Library Personnel Resources, 78
  Policy No. 106.11, 83
Anastasi, Joe, 28, 35
Andrews, Catherine, 74
Antidiscrimination Laws, 84–86, 89, 92–94

Age Discrimination in Employment Act of 1967, 6, 71, 79, 81
Civil Rights Act of 1964, 6, 74, 78, 81–83, 85, 90
Equal Opportunity Act of 1972, 78
Equal Pay Act of 1963, 6, 65, 79, 81, 88
Fair Labor Standards Act of 1938, 79
National Labor Relations Act, 81, 95, 100
OFCCP Order No. 4, 81
OFCCP Revised Order No. 14, 82
Ohio Fair Employment Practices Act, 93
Presidential Executive Orders
  10988, 101
  11246, 78–79, 81–82
  11375, 78–79, 81–82
  11141, 78–79
  11478, 78–79, 81
  11758, 78–79, 81
Rehabilitation Act Amendments of 1974, 79, 80, 82
Application Forms, 85–87, 92–93, 125–128
Arbitration, 97–98, 101, 104
Archuleta, Alyce, 65–66, 73, 91
Arvey, Richard D., 91
Association for Educational Communication and Technology, 114
Authority, 37–38, 40

B

Baird, John E., Jr., 30, 34
Baker, D. Phillip, 109, 114
Barber, Raymond W., 117
Baum, Fred, 74
Beacham, Samuel T., 71
Becker, J., 8
Bellasai, M., 21, 24
Berg, J. G., 68–70, 72
Bibliographic specialists, 2
Bingham, Rebecca T., 110, 114
Bittel, Lester R., 38, 40–41
Board of Trustees, 6–7, 11, 17–19, 22–23, 25, 31, 47, 51, 70–71, 98, 101–102
Boaz, Martha, 115
Bock, D. Joleen, 106, 108, 114
Bookmobile, 4
Book Talks, 45
Brandwein, Larry, 62, 100
Brooklyn Public Library, 62, 100
Brookmire, David A., 90
Brown, Geoff, 19, 24
Budgets, 3, 6–7, 22, 28, 43, 53, 66–67, 70–71, 96, 109–111, 114, 116, 118
Byam, Milton S., 97–98, 100

C

Career Ladder, 7
Carroll, Stephen J., 62, 71, 74
Carson, Ben, 106, 108–109, 111, 117
Carter, E. A., 31, 34
Censorship, 110
Change
  Library Education, 4
  Political, 5
  Management, 11, 23, 38, 40, 47
  Technological, 43
  Social, 43, 55
  Library Programs, 54, 98
Civil Rights Act
  (*See* Antidiscrimination Laws)
Civil Service
  Classification, 68

U.S. Commission, 80–81
Coaching, 44, 46, 48–50, 60, 62–63
Collective Bargaining, 95–96, 98–104
College Library
  (*See* Academic Library)
Communications, 2, 13–14, 23–24, 27–28, 30, 32, 35, 39–40, 50, 60, 63, 71, 106, 108
  Barriers, 29
  Written, 33
  Nonverbal, 34
Community Needs Assessment, 7, 21, 47–48, 51, 59
Compensation, 65–66, 69, 71–72, 74–76, 78, 79
  Benefits, 54, 77, 83, 88, 95–99, 102, 104
  Bonuses, 79
  Commissions, 79
  Increases, 58, 69, 71–73, 76, 79
  Overtime, 79
  Pay, 5, 7, 57, 64–66, 68–71, 75, 79, 83, 88–89, 91, 95, 97
  Salaries, 3, 22, 40, 55, 60, 65–66, 70, 73–75, 87, 91, 96–99, 102, 104, 117
  Salary Administration, 73, 75
Comprehensive Employment & Training Act, 103
Computers, 1–2, 4, 43, 48–49, 107
Conroy, Barbara, 53
Continuing Education, 53–55, 107, 110
  Conferences, 44–45, 99, 102
  Courses, 5, 43–45, 52
  Orientation, 52, 103
  Seminars, 1, 5, 44–45, 50, 55
  Workshops, 1, 5, 43–45, 47, 49, 50, 99, 115
Cooper, B. S., 100
Costs, 67
  Information Storage, 1
  Library Operation, 3, 22
  Management, 14
  Continuing Education, 44, 51, 53
  Materials, 108

Cost-of-Living, 66–67, 69, 71, 75, 96
Counseling, 23, 44, 60, 119
Courses, Academic
  (*See* Continuing Education)
Crisler, E., 113, 115
Cuesta, Yolanda, 84, 90
Cunningham, John, 90
Curriculum, 115–117
  Committee, 106, 108, 114
  Development, 105, 108–109, 114, 118
  Planning, 21

D

Dane, Chase, 107–108, 115
Darling, Richard L., 115
Decision-Making, 2, 12–13, 17, 23–24, 32, 45, 63, 95, 97, 102, 115
Delegation, 20, 24, 37–38, 45
Department of Labor
  U.S., 81
Desatnick, Robert L., 69, 72
Dickinson, Elizabeth, 78, 83, 90
Dipboye, Robert L., 86, 91
Discharge, 77–78, 88, 97
  Termination, 83, 87–88, 92–93, 101
Discipline, 77, 88, 92, 97
Discrimination, 72, 84–86, 89, 92–93
  Age, 77, 79, 83–84, 86–87, 93
  Color, 77–80, 83–85
  Handicap, 77, 79, 83–84, 86
  In Employment, 6, 77–78, 81, 90
  National Origin, 77–80, 82–86
  Race, 77–80, 83–87, 93
  Religion, 77–80, 82, 84–86, 93
  Sex, 65, 77–80, 82–85, 87, 91, 93
  Wage, 74, 91
District Media Supervision, 21, 50, 106, 115–116, 119
Dougherty, Richard M., 53
Downes, Valerie J., 116
Drucker, Peter F., 8, 58

E

Elementary & Secondary Education Act, 106
Emery, Richard, 33–34
Equal Employment Opportunity, 5, 6, 74, 77, 83, 87, 94
  Enforcement Agencies, 80, 81
  Laws (*See* Antidiscrimination Laws)
Equal Employment Opportunity Commission
  Federal, 7, 65, 74, 78, 80, 82, 87, 89, 90
Equal Opportunity Act
  (*See* Antidiscrimination Laws)
Equal Pay Act
  (*See* Antidiscrimination Laws)
Evaluation, 21, 24, 53, 57–58, 61, 69, 76, 106, 119
Forms, 76
Materials, 111

F

Facilitators, Learning, 5, 13–14, 107, 118
Facsimile Transmission, 2
Faculty Status, 76, 104
Fear, 27–29, 35, 41
Federal Privacy Act of 1974, 86
Firing
  (*See* Discharge)
Fite, Alice E., 106, 116
Fleuter, Douglas L., 72
Frantz, John C., 101
Free Access, 3
Friends of the Library, 21, 51
Fringe Benefits
  (*See* Compensation)

G

Galloway, Sue, 65–66, 73, 88, 91
Galvin, Thomas J., 115–116
Gambill, Ted R., 73
Gery, G. J., 91

Goldstein, Melvin S., 101
Grazier, Margaret H., 108, 116
Griffin, Richard E., 74
Guy, Jeniece, 97, 101

H

Hackman, J. Richard, 54
Hammer, Tove H., 91
Handicapped
  Students, 107
  Users, 4
  Workers, 6, 77, 85
Hargreaves, John, 31, 34
Hay System, 69
Heim, Kathleen M., 66, 73
Higgins, James M., 78, 92
Hilton, Robert C., 63
Hiring, 67, 77–78, 82–83, 85, 91–93, 97, 101, 119
  Ratio, 89
Hitt, William D., 60, 63
Hoban, Mary F., 66, 74
Human Relations, 35, 41
Human Resources, 1, 12, 43, 52–53, 55, 72

I

Independent Learning, 107
Inflation, 1, 3, 71, 75
Information and Referral
  Services, 50
Information Science, 4
Instant Information, 1
Intellectual Freedom, 33
Interlibrary Cooperation, 2, 23, 25, 109, 111, 115
Interpersonal Relationships, 17–18, 37, 39, 72, 105
Interviews, 48, 60, 84–85, 86, 91, 93
Issues
  Library, 5, 65
  Social, 5–6

J

Jaffe, Martin E., 101
Job Assignment, 77

Job Classification, 66–67, 69, 74, 78, 82–83
Job Description, 67–70, 86
Job Design, 54
Job Evaluation, 68, 72
Job Performance, 12, 18, 27, 30, 37, 43–46, 54, 57, 59, 62–63, 67, 69–70, 73, 75, 85–86, 88, 109, 113, 118
Job Responsibilities, 7, 18–19, 61
Job Rotation, 44
Job Security, 95, 97–98, 102
Josefowitz, N., 41

K

Kacena, Carolyn, 66, 73
Kaser, David, 43, 53
Kass, Tina, 66, 76
Kennelly, Jean R., 95, 97, 99, 102
Kimmel, Margaret M., 115–116
Kleingartner, Archie, 95, 97, 99, 102
Knapp School Libraries Project, 106, 116

L

Labor Relations, 95
Labor Unions, 6, 58, 62, 78–81, 95–104
  American Federation of School
    Administrators, 100
  American Federation of State,
    County, and Municipal
    Employees, 96
  Costs, 97, 100
  Librarians' Guild of the Civil Service Association, 103
  Women Library Workers, 65
Lawler, Edward E., 54
Layoffs, 58, 60, 83, 87
Leach, Daniel E., 65, 74
Leadership, 11, 17, 18, 52, 108, 110, 114
Learning Center
  (*See* School Library Media
  Center)
Levinson, H., 30, 35, 41

Library Cooperatives, 23, 47-48
  Multitype, 23
Librarians' Guild of the Civil Service Association
  (*See* Labor Unions)
Library Education, 1, 4, 8, 65, 75-76, 84, 97
  Faculty, 5
  Teaching, 45
Library Governance, 93-94, 97-98, 100
Library Media Specialist, 19, 21, 65-66, 96, 98-99, 105-107, 109-114, 116-119
Library School Faculty, 5, 74
Library Services, 1, 3, 7, 23-25, 31, 54, 100, 112
  Adult, 47, 49
  Children, 47, 49
  Home Delivery, 1
  Older Adults, 4
  Young Adults, 47, 119
Library Services and Construction Act, 115
Library Systems, 8
Library Technology
  (*See* Technology)
Lifelong Learning, 109
Likert, Rensis, 13-14
Listening, 28, 35, 44, 119
Little, Robert D., 105, 116
Lorey, Will, 27, 35

M

Mace, Wyles L., 46, 53
McCaskey, Michael B., 30, 35
McGregor, Douglas, 12, 14, 57, 60, 63
Management, 8, 14, 42, 100
  By Objectives, 58-60, 63, 117
  Of Self, 17, 19-20, 37
  Philosophy, 11-12, 63, 94
  Styles, 13-15
  Time, 19-20, 22-24, 32-33, 37, 62, 106
Mancall, Jacqueline C., 117

Martell, Charles R., 53
Martin, Betty, 106, 108-109, 111, 117
Maslow, Abraham, 12, 14
Mayer, Albert I., 98, 102
Mediation, 101
Menninger, William C., 30, 35, 41
Mentor, 44
Michener, Roger E., 96, 102
Microforms, 2
Military Service, 85
Minimum Wage, 67
Miniter, John J., 77, 92
Minorities, 6, 77-78, 81-91, 94
Mitnick, Margery M., 84, 88, 92
Mollenhoff, David V., 63
Mood, Lester F., 83, 93
Morale, 27, 31, 33, 35, 53, 70-71
Morano, Richard A., 64
Motivation, 12, 14, 34, 40, 63, 69-70, 74-75, 90, 112, 114
Musmann, Klaus, 54

N

Nash, A. N., 71, 74
National Defense Education Act, 106
National Education Association, 96
National Labor Relations Board, 81
National Library Week, 44
National Metal Trades Association, 69
Negotiations
  Labor-Management, 97, 101-102
Networks, 109, 111
Newsletters, 33-34
Nonprofessionals, 2, 3, 8, 37, 48, 67-69, 97, 103
Norwalk (CT) Public Library, 97, 103

O

Odiorne, George S., 54
Office of Federal Contracts Compliance Programs, 80, 82, 89

Ohio Civil Rights Commission, 85, 93
Omahan, Mary K., 86–87, 93
On-Line Services, 28, 46
Organizing
 Work, 21–22

P

Palmour, Vernon E., 21, 24
Pay
 (*See* Compensation)
Performance Appraisal, 44, 46, 57–64, 71–73, 83, 88, 113
 Form, 121–124
Personal Development, 58, 61–62, 72, 87
Pharaoh, Amenhotep, 11
Photocopying, 2, 23
Piamonte, John S., 69, 75
Planning
 Budget, 22
 Daily, 20
 Management, 43
 Process, 24, 58
 Program, 22, 106, 108
 Salary, 65–66, 70–71
 Work, 21, 24, 41, 59–61, 111
Planning Commission, 21
Point Factor Plan, 69, 72
Policies, 19
 Personnel, 6, 17, 52, 62, 89, 112
 Operating, 25, 30, 33, 109, 118
 Selection, 110, 118
Porter, Lyman W., 54
Principal, 19, 21, 23, 100, 106, 108–109, 115–119
Problem Solving, 58, 61–63, 71, 110, 116
Procedures
 Personnel, 17, 92, 101
 Operating, 33, 112
 Grievance, 102, 104
Productivity, 13–14, 27, 30, 35, 63, 76, 92
Professional Librarian, 2, 8, 22, 37, 49, 63, 66–67, 84, 102, 105, 111, 121

Professionalism, 6, 8, 37
Promotions, 5, 6, 46–47, 57–58, 60–62, 67, 76–78, 81, 83, 87, 89, 97, 109
Public Libraries, 3, 8, 21–24, 43, 47, 66–68, 73, 96–97, 100–101, 105, 115

Q

Qualifications
 Staff, 22
Questionnaires, 21
Quick, Thomas L., 13–14

R

Ranking, 68, 72
Rating, 58, 62, 109
 Forms, 60, 62
 Merit, 58
 Scale, 57
Recall, 87
Recognition, 33, 40, 66, 69, 72–73, 75
 Certificates, 113
Recruitment, 6, 72, 77–78, 83–84, 89, 92
Reference Checks, 85–87, 91–92
Research, 45
Resource Sharing, 3, 23, 106, 109
Retention
 Of Workers, 58, 72
Rewards, 2, 14, 64, 66–67, 69, 73, 75–76, 113
Rock, Milton, 75
Rogers, Carl, 107, 118
Rosenberg, Marc J., 109, 118
Rudy, M., 93

S

Salaries
 (*See* Compensation)
San Diego Public Library, 66
San Francisco Public Library, 97, 103
Schachat, Robert, 28, 35

Schedule, 20–21, 28, 32–33, 37–38, 60–61, 85, 106
Schiller, Anita 84, 94
Schlipf, Frederick A., 100, 102
School Librarian
(*See* Library Media Specialist)
School Library/Media Center, 3, 21–23, 43, 50, 67, 98–99, 105–106, 108–110, 112, 114–118
Learning Center, 107
Schweitzer, Albert, 18
Selection
Personnel, 83–87, 90–91, 93, 119,
Materials Policy, 110
Self-Actualization, 13
Self-Esteem, 2
Self-Fulfillment, 2, 71
Self-Realization, 69
Self-Instruction, 4, 44
Seniority, 58, 97, 103
Shaughnessy, Thomas W., 17, 24
Sinclair, Dorothy, 19, 24
Sinetar, Marsha, 9, 40, 42, 69, 75
Slanker, Barbara, 65, 75
Smith, Nathan M., 119
Special Library, 8, 21–23, 43, 49, 66–67, 69, 99, 105
Special Libraries Association, 66, 74–75
Staff Development, 2, 6–7, 12, 22, 37, 43, 45, 52–53, 55, 57, 63, 97, 106, 110–111, 113, 117, 119
Costs, 51
Planning, 46–48, 53
Staff Meetings, 23, 32
Staff Needs
Self-Esteem, 2
Self-Fulfillment, 2
Rewards, 2
Standards
Library, 8, 24–25
Library Media Center, 21, 106, 109, 116
Performance, 18, 40, 58, 61, 63, 67, 72
Stanton, Vida C., 112, 119
Stone, Elizabeth W., 55
Story Hours, 49, 58

Strack, Robert C., 110, 119
Stress, 13, 28, 30
Students, 4, 5, 19, 48, 105–108, 110, 112, 114, 119
Assistants, 113, 115
Gifted, 107
Student-Centered Teaching, 118
Subject Specialists, 1, 2, 5, 7, 66, 76, 111
Supervisor, 29, 30, 32–33, 35, 37–41, 44–48, 50, 55, 57–63, 72, 84, 90–92, 94, 97, 99, 100–101, 114

T

Taft-Hartley Act
(*See* Antidiscrimination Laws—National Labor Relations Act)
Task Force
Staff, 21, 59, 71
Teachers, 19, 21, 66, 96, 98–100, 105–106, 108–111, 114–115, 117, 119
Technology, 1–5, 24, 43, 54
Technical Information, 8
Television, 4
Tenure, 104
Termination
(*See* Discharge)
Terpstra, David E., 91
Tests, 83, 86
Theory X, 12
Theory Y, 12–13
Time Management
(*See* Management)
Tosi, Henry L., 62
Tracy, William R., 29, 36
Training, 1, 17, 20, 41, 43–46, 48, 52–55, 57, 60–62, 77–78, 83, 87, 90, 92, 97, 103, 112–113, 115
(*See also* Continuing Education)
Transfers, 83, 87, 97
Troubled Employee, 30
Turnover, 14, 27, 35, 53, 67

U

Unemployment, 86
User Fees, 7-8
Users, 2, 4, 19, 21
  Preschool Children, 109
  Senior Citizens, 109

V

Values
  Life, 19, 40
  Work, 8, 14, 42, 75
Volunteers, 3, 67, 105, 111-113, 115, 119

W

Wage Factors, 66
Wage Levels, 67
Warren, Malcolm W., 43, 55
Weatherford, John, 103
Weber, David C., 55, 66, 76
Wells, E. F., 18
White, Brenda H., 115-116
Wieting, Gretchen K., 34
Women, 6, 7, 41, 65, 73-74, 77, 81-84, 86-91, 94
Women Library Workers
  (*See* Labor Unions)
Working Conditions, 95, 97, 102

Y

Yen-Ran Yeh, Thomas, 76
Young, Virginia C., 101